# JOSIAH'S RE

# JOSIAH'S REFORMATION

## Richard Sibbes

*For thus saith the high and lofty One that inhabiteth eternity, whose Name is Holy; I dwell in the high and holy place, with him also that is of a contrite and humble spirit, to revive the spirit of the humble, and to revive the heart of the contrite ones.*
Isaiah 57:15

## THE BANNER OF TRUTH TRUST

THE BANNER OF TRUTH TRUST
3 Murrayheld Road, Edinburgh EH12 6EL, UK
P.O. Box 621, Carlisle, PA 17013, USA

*

First published 1629 as part of *The Saint's Cordials*

Previously published in
*The Works of Richard Sibbes*, vol. 6
(1862-4; repr. Banner of Truth Trust, 1983)

This edition first published 2011
© The Banner of Truth Trust, 2011

ISBN: 978 1 84871 116 7

*

Typeset in 11/15 pt Sabon Oldstyle Figures
at the Banner of Truth Trust, Edinburgh

Printed in the USA by
Versa Press, Inc.,
East Peoria, IL

# Contents

# FOREWORD

Richard Sibbes (1577-1635)—the 'heavenly Doctor' as he came to be called—was a man who clearly enjoyed knowing God. And even centuries later, his relish is infectious. He spoke of the living God as a life-giving, warming sun who 'delights to spread his beams and his influence in inferior things, to make all things fruitful. Such a goodness is in God as is in a fountain, or in the breast that loves to ease itself of milk.'[1]

And knowing God to be such an overflowing fountain of goodness and love made him a most attractive model of God-likeness. For, he said, 'those that are led with the Spirit of God, that are like him; they have a communicative, diffusive goodness that loves to spread itself.'[2] In other words, knowing God's love,

---

[1] *Works of Richard Sibbes,* 7 vols., Alexander B. Grosart, ed., (Edinburgh, 1862-1864; reprint ed., Edinburgh: Banner of Truth, 1973-1982), 6:113.

[2] *Ibid.,* 6:113.

he became loving; and his understanding of who God is transformed him into a man, a preacher, and a writer of magnetic geniality. He was never married, but looking at his life, it is clear that he had a quite extraordinary ability for cultivating warm and lasting friendships. Charles Spurgeon once told his students that he loved the sort of minister whose face invites you to be his friend, the sort of face on which you read the sign 'Welcome' and not 'Beware of the dog'. He could have been describing Sibbes.

Sibbes was born to a wheelwright in a rather obscure little village in Suffolk. Few could have expected how influential the young man would turn out to be. Before long, though, it was clear that he was remarkably capable: sailing through his studies at Cambridge, he became a tutor at St John's College aged only twenty-four. Bright as he was, though, it was his ability as a preacher that soon began to mark him out. Before long, he was appointed to be a 'lecturer' at Holy Trinity Church in Cambridge (where a gallery had to be built to accommodate the extra numbers he attracted), and a few years later he was appointed to be a preacher at Gray's Inn, one of the London Inns of Court where many soon-to-be-influential men of Puritan persuasion came to hear him.

Knowing, as he once said, that there is more grace in Christ than there is sin in us, he always sought in his preaching to win the hearts of his listeners to Christ. This, he believed, was the special duty of ministers: 'they woo for Christ, and open the riches, beauty, honour, and all that is lovely in him.'[3] The result was preaching so winsome that struggling believers began to call him the 'honey-mouthed', the 'sweet dropper', and, apparently, hardened sinners deliberately avoided his sermons for fear he would convert them. One listener, Humphrey Mills, recorded his experience of Sibbes's ministry, and it seems to have been typical:

I was for three years together wounded for sins, and under a sense of my corruptions, which were many; and I followed sermons, pursuing the means, and was constant in duties and doing; looking for Heaven that way. And then I was so precise for outward formalities, that I censured all to be reprobates, that wore their hair anything long, and not short above their ears; or that wore great ruffs, and gorgets, or fashions, and follies. But yet I was distracted in my mind, wounded in conscience, and wept often and bitterly, and prayed earnestly, but yet had no comfort, till I heard that sweet saint . . . Doctor Sibbs, by whose means and ministry I was brought to peace and joy in my spirit. His sweet soul-melting Gospel-sermons won my heart and refreshed me much, for by him I saw and had much of God and was confident in Christ, and could overlook

[3] *Ibid.*, 2:24.

the world . . . my heart held firm and resolved and my desires all heaven-ward.[4]

In 1626, Sibbes was appointed Master of Katharine Hall, Cambridge, and for the last decade of his life he would use his considerable influence to promote his Christ-centred theology. He sought to place trusted Puritan preachers in church teaching posts around the country; he personally nurtured a number of young ministers, men such as Thomas Goodwin, John Cotton, Jeremiah Burroughs, John Preston, and Philip Nye; and through his printed sermons he affected countless more.

Richard Sibbes was not the first Puritan I read (I started with John Owen), but to my mind Sibbes is actually the best introduction to the Puritans. And ever since the day when, as a student, I read his *The Bruised Reed,* Sibbes has been my favourite. 'Sibbes never wastes the student's time,' wrote Spurgeon, 'he scatters pearls and diamonds with both hands.' Reading him is like sitting in the sunshine: he gets into your heart and warms it to Christ.

This book was originally a four-part sermon series on 2 Chronicles 34:26-28, where the Lord is said to have heard Josiah because his heart was tender, because he was humble and because he mourned his sin.

---

[4] John Rogers, *Ohel or Bethshemesh, A Tabernacle for the Sun* (London, 1653), 410.

The first sermon, 'The Tender Heart', is founda-
tional, not only for the rest of the series, but for all of
Sibbes's theology. In his ministry, Sibbes always sought
to get under the superficial layer of his listeners' behaviour and deal with their hearts, their affections and
their desires. For Sibbes, this was no secondary matter, the devotional clothes his theology wore. Rather,
in looking to deal with the heart, he believed he was
preserving one of the most profound insights of the
Reformation of which he was a part.

Again and again in his sermons, Sibbes speaks of
both Catholic priests and Protestant pastors who—
whatever their professed theology—act as though the
root of our problem before God lies in our behaviour:
we have done wrong things and we need to start doing
right things. Sibbes plumbs much deeper. He knew
that the outward acts of sin are merely the manifesta-
tions of the inner desires of the heart. Merely to alter a
person's behaviour without dealing with those desires
would cultivate hypocrisy, the self-righteous cloak for a
cold and vicious heart. And, Sibbes would note, minis-
tries that worked like that were invariably cruel, based
on brow-beating. No, hearts must be turned, and evil
desires eclipsed by stronger ones for Christ.

In 'The Tender Heart', then, Sibbes sets about the
deepest possible work—of heart-surgery. He explains
that those who are tender-hearted—who are soft to the

Lord—do not simply desire 'salvation'; they desire the Lord of salvation himself. Only then, when a person is brought to love the Lord with heart-felt sincerity, will they truly begin to hate their sin instead of merely dreading the thought of God's punishment of it. In all this, Sibbes displays just how beautiful, pure, and desirable a soft heart is, and by his honesty and kindness, he heaps burning coals on hypocrisy, making you mourn your own hard-heartedness as you feel what a wretched thing it is.

Then, having whetted your appetite for such a heart, he shows you how hearts can be made tender:

> Tenderness of heart is wrought by an apprehension of tenderness and love in Christ. A soft heart is made soft by the blood of Christ. (p. 13 below)

> As when things are cold we bring them to the fire to heat and melt, so *bring we our cold hearts to the fire of the love of Christ.* (p. 35 below)

> If thou wilt have this tender and melting heart, then *use the means* [of grace]; be always under the sunshine of the gospel. (p. 35 below)

Not only is Sibbes beautifully capturing the warmth and joy of hearty holiness; he is also making a most significant point. That is, we are sanctified just as we were first saved—through believing in Christ. By revealing

Christ to me, the Spirit turns my heart from its natural hatred of God towards a sincere love for him. Only thereby can my heart be made tender. Sibbes once said to Thomas Goodwin, 'Young man, if ever you would do good, you must preach the gospel and the free grace of God in Christ Jesus.' He meant it with every fibre of his being, for he saw that the free grace of God in Christ Jesus is the means by which the hearts of sinners are first turned to God, and the means by which the hearts of believers continue to be turned from the love of sin to love of God.

I don't think I can exaggerate the importance of 'The Tender Heart' and its message for today. Our busyness and activism so easily degenerate into a hypocrisy in which we keep up all the appearance of holiness without the heart of it. Ministers can bludgeon their people into such hollow Christianity, and even use Christ as a package to pass on to others, instead of enjoying him first and foremost as their own Saviour. But true Reformation—whether Reformation in Josiah's day, Sibbes's, or ours—must begin in the heart, with love for Christ. And that can only come when the free grace of God in Christ Jesus is preached.

After 'The Tender Heart', the next two sermons unpack what such a heart will be like. In 'The Art of Self-Humbling', Sibbes shows that tenderness of heart and humility go together. And that is because humility is not the vain attempt to think less of myself (which would simply be a masochistic form of self-obsession); it is the inevitable result of having a softened heart. The hard-hearted, captivated by themselves, proudly revel in their supposed independence and strength. But with my heart won to the Lord, and ever more captivated by him, I begin to revel in my absolute dependence on him. For, recognising my emptiness, I now love God's glorious fullness. So 'Grow in the love of God' (p. 72 below) Sibbes counsels those who would have a hearty humility.

In the third sermon, 'The Art of Mourning' (by which he means mourning for sin), Sibbes explains how the heart that grows to love the Lord grows to hate sin. A hard heart simply cannot feel the weight of the sin it bears, and so while hypocrites may battle with their sin for how it discredits them, they will never truly hate it. But again, it is only a hearty mourning for sin that Sibbes is interested in.

> The outward is easy, and subject to hypocrisy. It is an easy matter to rend clothes and to force tears, but it is a hard matter to afflict the soul. The heart of man taketh the easiest ways, and lets the hardest alone, thinking to please God with that. But God will not be served so; for he must have the inward affections, or else he doth abhor the outward actions. (pp. 88-89 below)

Occasionally, some have suspected Sibbes of sentimentalism. All this talk of heart-felt desires, of affections for the Lord, of tears for sin: is this soppy Christianity? For such censors, Sibbes has the most damning rebuke. It is, he says, no weak ('womanish') thing to love the Lord so; to suggest that it is, simply reveals a repulsive cold-heartedness, a proud and faithless desire to be strong in ourselves.

Appropriately, Sibbes concludes the work with 'The Saint's Refreshing', in which he unfolds the tender heart's much-desired reward: we shall be gathered to Christ!

Richard Sibbes was a bright lantern of the Reformation, and he knew the issues dealt with in this book to be essential to the work of reform. Oh, may it reform you as you read it, and foster reformation in our day!

MICHAEL REEVES
Oxford
January 2011

# I

## THE TENDER HEART

*And as for the king of Judah, who sent you to inquire
of the Lord, so shall ye say unto him, Thus saith the
Lord God of Israel concerning the words which thou
hast heard, Because thine heart was tender, etc.*

2 Chron. 34:26–27

THESE words are a part of the message which the
prophetess Huldah sent to good King Josiah; for
as the message was concerning him and his people,
so his answer from her is exact, both for himself
and them. That part which concerned his people is
set down in the three foregoing verses; that which
belongs unto himself is contained in the words now
read unto you, 'But to the king of Judah, *etc.*' The
preface to her message we see strengthened with

authority from God, 'Thus saith the Lord God of Israel'; which words carry in them the greater force and power from the majesty of the author. For if words spoken from a king carry authority, how much more then the word of the Lord of hosts, the King of kings? Here is her wisdom, therefore, that she lays aside her own authority, and speaks in the name of the Lord.

We see that waters of the same colour have not the same nature and effect, for hot waters are of the same colour with plain ordinary waters, yet more effectual; so the words of a man coming from a man may seem at first to be the same with others, yet notwithstanding, the words of God, coming from the Spirit of God, carry a more wonderful excellency in them even to the hearts of kings. They bind kings, though they labour to shake them off. They are arrows to pierce their hearts; if not to save them, yet to damn them. Therefore she speaks to the king, 'Thus saith the Lord God of Israel concerning the words which thou hast heard, *etc.*'

Here we read of Josiah, that he was a man of an upright heart, and one who did that which was right in the sight of the Lord; and answerably we find the Lord to deal with him. For he, desirous to know the issue of a fearful judgment threatened against him and his people, sendeth to Huldah, a prophetess of the Lord, to be certified therein; whereupon he receiveth a full and perfect answer of the Lord's determination, both touching himself and his people, that they being forewarned might be forearmed; and by a timely conversion to the Lord, might procure the aversion[1] of so heavy wrath. He in uprightness sends to inquire, and the Lord returns him a full and upright answer. Whence we may learn,

*Doct.* 1. *That God doth graciously fit prophets for persons, and his word to a people that are upright in their hearts.* Where there is a true desire to know the will of God, there God will give men sincere prophets that shall answer them exactly; not according to their own lusts, but for their good. Josiah was an holy man, who, out of a gracious disposition, desirous to be informed from God what should become of him and his people, sends to the prophetess Huldah. It was God's mercy that he should have a Huldah, a Jeremiah, to send to; and it was God's mercy that they should deal faithfully with him. This is God's mercy to those that are true-hearted. He will give them teachers suitable to their desires; but those that are false-hearted shall have suitable teachers, who shall instruct them according to their lusts. If

---

[1] That is, 'turning away'.

3

they be like Ahab, they shall have four hundred false prophets to teach falsehood, to please their lusts (*1 Kings* 22:6); but if they be Davids, they shall have Nathans. If they be Josiahs, they shall have Huldahs and Jeremiahs. Indeed, Herod may have a John Baptist (*Mark* 6:17–27); but what will he do with him in the end when he doth come to cross him in his sin? Then off goes his head.

*Use.* This should teach us to labour for sincerity, to have our hearts upright towards God; and then he will send us men of a direct and right spirit, that shall teach us according to his own heart. But if we be false-hearted, God will give us teachers that shall teach us, not according to his will, but to please our own. We shall light upon belly-gods and epicures, and shall fall into the hands of priests and Jesuits. Where such are, there are the judgments of God upon the people, because they do not desire to know the will of God in truth. We see (*Ezek.* 14:3, 4), the people desired to have a stumblingblock for their iniquity. They were naught,[2] and would have idols. Therefore they desired stumblingblocks. They would have false prophets, that so they might go to hell with some authority. Well, saith God, they shall have stumblingblocks: for thus saith the Lord

---

[2] That is, 'naughty', wicked.

God of Israel, 'To every man that setteth up his idols in his heart, and putteth the stumblingblock of his iniquity before his face, and cometh to the prophet to inquire; I the Lord will answer him that cometh, according to the multitude of his idols; according to his own false heart, and not according to good.' What brought the greatest judgment upon the world, next to hell itself, I mean antichrist—the terriblest judgment of all, that hath drawn so many souls to hell—but the wickedness of the place and people, and his own ambition? The sins of the people gave life to him. They could not endure the word of God or plain dealing; they thought it a simple thing. They must have more sacrifices, more ceremonies, and a more glorious government. They would not be content with Christ's government which he left them, but were weary of this. Therefore, he being gone to heaven, they must have a pope to go before them and lead them to hell. Therefore let men never excuse those sins, for certainly God saw a great deal of evil in them and therefore gave them up to the judgment of antichrist. But let us magnify God's mercies that hath not so given us up. Thus we see how graciously God deals with a true-hearted king: he sends him a true answer of his message.

Verse 27, 'Because thine heart was tender, *etc.*'

Now here comes a comfortable message to good Josiah, that he should be taken away and not see the miseries that should befall his people; the cause whereof is here set down, 'Because thy heart was tender and thou didst humble thyself before God'; which cause is double.

1. *Inward.*

2. *Outward.*

1. The inward is the tenderness of his heart and humbling of himself. 2. And then, the outward expression of it is set down in a double act:

(1.) Rending of clothes. (2.) Weeping.

'Because thou hast rent thy clothes, and wept before me.' After which comes the promise, 'I have also heard thee,' saith the Lord; 'behold, I will gather thee to thy fathers, and thou shalt be put in thy grave in peace, and thine eyes shall not see all the evil which I will bring upon this place, and upon the inhabitants of the same.'

I will first remove one doubt, before I come to the tenderness of Josiah's heart.

*Quest.* What! may some say, Is there anything in man that can cause God to do him good?

*Ans.* No. One thing is the cause of another, but all come from the first cause. So tenderness of heart may be some cause of removal of judgment; but God is the cause of both, for they all come from the first cause: which is God. So that these words do rather contain an order than a cause. For God hath set down this order in things, that where there is a broken heart there shall be a freedom from judgment; not that tenderness of heart deserves anything at God's hand, as the papists gather, but because God hath decreed it so, that where tenderness of heart is, there mercy shall follow; as here there was a tender heart in Josiah, therefore mercy did follow. God's promises are made conditionally; not that the condition on our part deserves anything at God's hand, but when God hath given the condition, he gives the thing promised. So that this is an order which God hath set down, that where there is grace, mercy shall follow. For where God intends to do any good, he first works in them a gracious disposition: after which he looks upon his own work as upon a lovely object, and so doth give them other blessings. God crowns grace with grace.

By 'heart' is not meant the inward material and fleshy part of the body; but that spiritual part, the soul and affections thereof. In that it is said to be 'tender' or melting, it is a borrowed and metaphorical phrase. Now in a ' tender heart' these three properties concur:

1. *It is sensible.* 2. *It is pliable.* 3. *It is yielding.*

1. First, A tender heart is always a *sensible*[3] heart. It hath life and therefore sense. There is no living creature but hath life, and sense to preserve that life. So a tender heart is sensible of any grievance, for tenderness doth presuppose life, because nothing that hath not life is tender. Some senses are not altogether necessary for the being of a living creature, as hearing and seeing; but sensibleness is needful to the being of every living creature. It is a sign of life in a Christian when he is sensible of inconveniences. Therefore God hath planted such affections in man, as may preserve the life of man, as fear and love. Fear is that which makes a man avoid many dangers. Therefore God hath given us fear to cause us make our peace with him in time, that we may be freed from inconveniences; yea, from that greatest of inconveniences, hell fire.

2, 3. Again, A tender heart is *pliable* and *yielding*. Now that is said to be yielding and pliable, which yields to the touch of anything that is put to it, and doth not stand out, as a stone that rebounds back when it is thrown against a wall. So that is said to be tender which hath life, and sense, and is pliable, as wax is yielding and pliable to the disposition of him

---

[3] That is, 'sensitive'.

that works it, and is apt to receive any impression that is applied to it. In a tender heart there is no resistance, but it yields presently to every truth, and hath a pliableness and a fitness to receive any impression, and to execute any performance; a fit temper indeed for a heart wrought on by the Spirit. God must first make us fit, and then use us to work. As a wheel must first be made round, and then turned round, so the head must be first altered, and then used in a renewed way. A tender heart, so soon as the word is spoken, yields to it. It quakes at threatenings, obeys precepts, melts at promises, and the promises sweeten the heart. In all duties concerning God, and all offices of love to men, a tender heart is thus qualified. But hardness of heart is quite opposite. For, as things dead and insensible, it will not yield to the touch, but returns back whatsoever is cast upon it. Such a heart may be broken in pieces, but it will not receive any impression; as a stone may be broken, but will not be pliable, but rebound back again. A hard heart is indeed like wax to the devil, but like a stone to God or goodness. It is not yielding, but resists and repels all that is good; and therefore compared in the Scripture to the adamant stone. Sometimes it is called a frozen heart, because it is unpliable to anything. You may break it in pieces, but it is unframeable for any service, for any impression; it will not be wrought upon. But on the contrary, a melting and tender heart is sensible, yielding, and fit for any service both to God and man. Thus we see plainly what a tender heart is. The point from hence is,

*Doct.* 2. *That it is a supernatural disposition of a true child of God to have a tender, soft, and a melting heart.* I say that a disposition of a true child of God and the frame of soul of such an one, to be tender, apprehensive, and serviceable, is a supernatural disposition; and of necessity it must be so, because naturally the heart is of another temper—a stony heart. All by nature have stony hearts in respect of spiritual goodness. There may be a tenderness in regard of natural things; but in regard of grace, the heart is stony, and beats back all that is put to it. Say what you will to a hard heart, it will never yield. A hammer will do no good to a stone. It may break it in pieces, but not draw it to any form. So to a stony heart, all the threatenings in the world will do no good. You may break it in pieces, but never work upon it. It must be the almighty power of God. There is nothing in the world so hard as the heart of man. The very creatures will yield obedience to God; as flies, and lice, to destroy Pharaoh; but Pharaoh himself was so hard-hearted, that after ten plagues he was ten times the more hardened (*Exod.* 10:27). Therefore, if a man have not a melting heart, he is diverted from his proper object; because God hath placed affections in us, to be raised presently upon suitable objects. When any object is offered in the word of God, if our hearts were not corrupted, we would have correspondent affections. At judgments we would tremble, at the word of threatenings quake, at promises we would with faith believe, and at mercies be comforted; at directions we would be pliable and yielding. But by nature our hearts are hard. God, may threaten, and promise, and direct, and yet we insensible all the while. Well, all Josiahs, and all that are gracious, of necessity must have soft hearts. Therefore I will show you,

1. *How a tender heart is wrought.*
2. *How it may be preserved and maintained.*
3. *How it may be discerned from the contrary.*

1. First, A tender heart is made tender *by him that made it*. For no creature in the world can soften and turn the heart, only God must alter and change it; for we are all by nature earthly, dead, and hard. Hence is it that God doth make that gracious promise, *Ezek.* 11:19, 'I will give them one heart, and put a new spirit within their bowels; and I will take away the stony

hearts out of their bodies, and give them a heart of flesh', that is a living, sensible heart.

*Quest.* But doth God immediately make the heart tender, and change it, without any help by means?

*Sol.* 1. I answer, Means do not make the heart tender, but God through the use of means softens it by his word. God's word is a hammer to break, and as fire to melt the hardened heart (*Jer.* 23:29). And thus it works, first, when God doth show to the heart our cursed estate, and opens to the same the true dangers of the soul, which it is in by nature and custom of sin, and sets before it the terrors of the last day and present danger of judgment. When the Spirit of God, by the word, doth convince the soul to be in a damned estate, dead, born under wrath, and an heir of damnation; that by nature God frowns, and hell is ready to swallow us up; when the soul is thus convinced, then the heart begins to be astonished and cries out, 'Men and brethren, what shall I do?' (*Acts* 2:37). When the word is thus preached with particular application, it doth good. For a man may hear the word of God generally, and yet have no broken heart. But when a Peter comes and saith, 'You have crucified the Lord of life'; and when a Nathan comes to David, and saith, 'Thou art the man', then comes the heart to be broken and confounded.

But it is not enough to have the heart broken; for a pot may be broken in pieces, and yet be good for nothing; so may a heart be, through terrors, and sense of judgment, and yet not be like wax, pliable. Therefore it must be melting;[4] for which cause, when God by his judgments hath cast down the heart, then comes the Spirit of God, revealing the comfort of the word; then the gracious mercy of God in Christ is manifested, that 'there is mercy with God, that he may be feared' (*Psa.* 130:4). This being laid open to the quick, to a dejected soul, hence it comes to be melted and tender; for the apprehension of judgment is only a preparing work, which doth break the heart, and prepare it for tenderness.

*Sol.* 2. Again, Tenderness of heart is wrought by an apprehension of tenderness and love in Christ. A soft heart is made soft by the blood of Christ. Many say, that an adamant cannot be melted with fire, but by blood. I cannot tell whether this be true or no; but I am sure nothing will melt the hard heart of man but the blood of Christ, the passion of our blessed Saviour. When a man considers of the love that God hath showed him in sending of his Son, and doing such great things as he hath done, in giving of Christ to satisfy his justice, in setting us free from hell,

---

[4] Or 'melted'.

Satan and death: the consideration of this, with the persuasion that we have interest in the same, melts the heart, and makes it become tender. And this must needs be so, because that with the preaching of the gospel unto broken-hearted sinners cast down, there always goes the Spirit of God, which works an application of the gospel.

Christ is the first gift to the church. When God hath given Christ, then comes the Spirit, and works in the heart a gracious acceptance of mercy offered. The Spirit works an assurance of the love and mercy of God. Now love and mercy felt, work upon the tender heart a reflective love to God again. What, hath the great God of heaven and earth sent Christ into the world for me? humbled himself to the death of the cross for me? and hath he let angels alone, and left many thousands in the world, to choose me? and hath he sent his ministers to reveal unto me this assurance of the love and mercy of God? This consideration cannot but work love to God again; for love is a kind of fire which melts the heart. So that when our souls are persuaded that God loves us from everlasting, then we reflect our love to him again; and then our heart says to God, 'Speak, Lord; what wilt thou have me to do?' The soul is pliable for doing, for suffering, for anything God will have it. Then, 'Speak, Lord, for thy servant heareth' (*1 Sam.* 3:9).

And when the heart is thus wrought upon, and made tender by the Spirit, then afterward in the proceeding of our lives, many things will work tenderness: as the works of God, his judgments, the word and sacraments, when they are made effectual by the Spirit of God, work tenderness. The promises of God also make the heart tender, as *Rom.* 12:1, 'I beseech you, brethren, by the mercies of God, offer up your souls and bodies a living sacrifice, holy and acceptable unto God.' There is no such like argument to persuade men to tenderness of heart, as to propound the love and mercy of God. And so the fear of any judgment will work tenderness. This made Josiah's heart to melt, but yet this did not work first upon him; for he having a tender heart before, and being sure of God's love, when he heard the judgment that should come upon his people, out of love to God and to his people, his heart melted, not so much for fear of judgment, but to think that God should be provoked by the sins of his people.

And thus we have seen how tenderness of heart is wrought. Now I come to show,

2. *Second, The means how we may preserve this tenderness of heart,* because it is a disposition of

God's children. How then shall we preserve ourselves in such a perpetual temper? The way to preserve a tender heart is,

1. First, *To be under the means whereby God's Spirit will work;* for it is he by his Spirit that works upon the heart, and doth preserve tenderness in us; and he will work only by his own means. All the devices in the world will not work upon the heart. Therefore let us be under the means that may preserve tenderness, and hear what God's word says of our estate by nature, of the wrath and justice of God, and of the judgment that will shortly come upon all the world. This made Paul to cry, though he knew that he was the child of God, and free from the law. 'Therefore', saith he, 'knowing the terror of the law, we admonish you' (2 *Cor.* 5:11).

2. And then, *go into the house of mourning, and present before yourselves the miserable and forlorn estate of the church of God abroad.* It was this that broke Nehemiah's heart. When he heard that the Jews were in great affliction and reproach, that the wall of the city was broken down, and the gates thereof burnt with fire, he sat down and wept, and mourned certain days, fasted and prayed before the God of heaven (*Neh.* 1:4). This made this good man Nehemiah to mourn, so that all the princes of the court

could not comfort him. This also made Moses's heart to melt, when he looked on his brethren's affliction in Egypt. So we might keep our hearts tender if we did but set before our eyes the pitiful estate of God's church abroad, and that we may come to be in such an estate ourselves ere long.

3. And if thou wilt preserve tenderness of heart, *labour for a legal and evangelical faith*. We must believe that all the threatenings of God's vengeance against the wicked shall come to pass. Faith doth make these things present before our eyes; for it is the nature of faith to set things absent as present before us. What makes the malefactor to tremble and be cast down, but when he sees that he is ready for to die, is going to the place of execution, and sees death look him in the face? So faith setting the day of judgment before our eyes, will make us to tremble. Therefore Paul doth so often adjure Timothy by the coming of the Lord Jesus to judgment, (2 *Tim.* 4:1); and Enoch set the day of judgment before him, at the beginning of the world, as we may see in *Jude* 14-15. He had a faith, that set things to come as present, and made him to walk with God. So if we had an evangelical faith to believe the goodness of God, pardon from him, and everlasting life, this would preserve tenderness of heart.

4. Again, *Good company will preserve tenderness of heart, sorting ourselves with those that are tender-hearted.* For the soul will reason thus: Doth such an one make conscience of swearing, profaning the Sabbath? and doth he mourn for the miseries of the church? Then what a hard piece of dead flesh am I, that have nothing in me!

5. Again, If thou wouldst preserve tenderness of heart, *by all means take heed of the least sin against conscience,* for the least sin in this kind makes way for hardness of heart. Sins that are committed against conscience do darken the understanding, dead the affection, and take away life; so that one hath not the least strength to withstand the least temptation. And so it comes to pass by God's judgment; for when men will live in sins against conscience, he takes away his Spirit, and gives up the heart from one degree of hardness to another. For the heart at first being tender, will endure nothing, but the least sin will trouble it. As water, when it begins to freeze, will not endure anything, no not so much as the weight of a pin upon it, but after a while will bear the weight of a cart; even so at the beginning, the heart being tender, trembles at the least sin, and will not bear with any one; but when it once gives way to sins against conscience, it becomes so frozen that it can endure

any sin, and so becomes more and more hard. Men are so obdurate, having once made a breach in their own hearts by sins against conscience, that they can endure to commit any sin; and therefore God gives them up from one degree of hardness to another. What will not men do whom God hath given up to hardness of heart?

6. Again, If thou wilt preserve tenderness of heart, *take heed of spiritual drunkenness;* that is, that thou be not drunk with an immoderate use of the creatures; of setting thy love too much upon outward things. For what saith the prophet? 'Wine and women take away the heart' (*Hos.* 4:11); that is, the immoderate use of any earthly thing takes away spiritual sense; for the more sensible the soul is of outward things, the less it is of spiritual. For as the outward takes away the inward heat, so the love of one thing abates the love of another. The setting of too much love upon earthly things, takes away the sense of better things, and hardens the heart. When the heart is filled with the pleasures and profits of this life, it is not sensible of any judgment that hangs over the head; as in the old world, 'they ate and drank, they married and gave in marriage, they bought and sold, while the flood came upon them and swept all away' (*Matt.* 24:38–39). When a man sets his love upon the

creature, the very strength of his soul is lost. Therefore in the Scripture, God joins prayer and fasting both together (*Matt.* 17:21); that when he would have our hearts raised up to heaven, we should have all use of earthly things taken away. Therefore when we are to go about spiritual duties, we must cut ourselves short in the use of the creatures. Talk of religion to a carnal man, whose senses are lost with love of earthly things, he hath no ear for that; his sense is quite lost, he hath no relish or savour of anything that is good. Talk to a covetous man, that hath his soul set upon the things of this life, he hath no relish of anything else; his heart is already so hardened to get honour and wealth, though it be to the ruin of others, that he cares not how hard it become. Therefore we are bidden to take heed that our hearts be not overcome with drunkenness and the cares of this life, for these will make a man to be insensible of spiritual things (*Luke* 21:34).

7. Again, If thou wilt preserve tenderness of heart, *take heed of hypocrisy;* for it causeth swelling, and pride makes the heart to contemn others that be not like unto us. They bless themselves that they live thus and thus, they think themselves better than any other; and if they hear the minister reprove them for sin, they will shift it off, and say, Oh, this belongeth not

to me, but to such a carnal man, and to such a wicked person; as the Scribes and Pharisees, who were vile hypocrites, yet they were the cause of all mischief, and more hard-hearted than Pilate, an heathen man; for he would have delivered Christ, but they would not (*Luke* 23:14–23). So, take a Romish hypocrite, that can proudly compliment it at every word with enticing speech, yet you shall find him more hard-hearted than Turk or Jew; for full of cruelty and blood is the 'whore of Babylon.' Therefore, if thou wilt have tenderness of heart, take heed of hypocrisy.

8. Again, Above all things, *take heed of great sins*, which will harden the heart; for little sins do many times not dead the heart, but stir up the conscience; but great sins do stond[5] and dull a man; as a prick of a pin will make a man to start, but a heavy blow maketh a man for to be dead for the present. Therefore take heed of great sins. Thus it was with David. He sinned in numbering of the people, and for this his heart smote him; but when he came to the great and devouring sin of Uriah and Bathsheba, this was a great blow that struck him and laid him for dead, till Nathan came and revived him (2 *Sam.* 12:1). For when men fall into great sins, their hearts are so hardened, that they go on from sin to sin.

---

[5] That is, 'stun', = harden.

Let us therefore be watchful over our own hearts, to preserve tenderness. The eye being a tender part, and soonest hurt, how watchful is man by nature over that, that it take no hurt. So the heart, being a tender thing, let us preserve it by all watchfulness to keep blows from off it. It is a terrible thing to keep a wound of some great sin upon the conscience, for it makes a way for a new breach; because when the conscience once begins to be hardened with some great sin, then there is no stop, but we run on to commit sin with all greediness.

9. Lastly, If thou wilt preserve tenderness of heart, *consider the miserable estate of hardness of heart.* Such an one that hath an hard heart is next to hell itself, to the estate of a damned spirit, a most terrible estate. A hard heart is neither melted with promises nor broken with threatenings. He hath no bowels of pity to men or love to God. He forgets all judgment for things past, and looks for none to come. When the soul is in this case, it is fit for nothing but for sin and the devil, whereas a tender-hearted man is fit for all good. Let God threaten: he trembles and quakes; let God promise: his heart melts and rejoiceth, and makes him even to break forth into thanksgiving; let God command: he will perform all; he is fit for any good thing to God and man. But when a man's heart

is hardened by hypocrisy, covetousness, or custom in sin, he hath no pity, no compassion: let God command, threaten, or promise, yet the heart is never a whit moved. This is a terrible estate of soul.

Now, to speak a little to *young men* that are like to this holy man Josiah.

Surely his tenderness had some advantage from his years. Let those that are young by all means labour to keep tenderness of heart; for if young persons be good, there is a sweet communion between God and them, before the heart be pestered with the cares of the world. God delights much in the prayers of young men, because they come not from so polluted a soul, hardened with the practices of this world. Let such, therefore, as are young, take advantage of it, to repent in time of their sins, and let them not put it off unto their old days. While we are young, let us not neglect natural tenderness; although we cannot bring ourselves under the compass of God's kingdom by it, yet shall we get our hearts the sooner to be tender. In our youth, therefore, let us not neglect this good opportunity, as good Josiah did not when he was but young. Therefore let us repent of every sin betimes, and acquaint ourselves with those that are good; as it is said (*Heb.* 3:13), 'Let us provoke one another daily, while it is called today, lest any of you be hardened through the deceitfulness of sin.' Let us use all means to keep our hearts tender. Oh, it is a blessed estate! We are fit to live when our hearts are tender; fit to die, fit to receive anything from God, fit for duties of honesty to men, for any service to God. But when we have lost sense and feeling, it must be the almighty power of God that must recover us again, and not one amongst an hundred comes to good. Therefore labour to preserve a tender, soft, and melting heart.

Now, ere I proceed, give me leave to answer some cases of conscience, as,

*Quest.* 1. First, Whether the children of God may be subject to this hardness of heart, opposed to this tenderness?

*Quest.* 2. Secondly, Whether a Christian may be more sensible of outward things than of spiritual, as the love of God, or his own sin, and the like?

*Sol.* 1. To the first I answer, *that the child of God may be hard-hearted*. He may have some degrees of hardness of heart in him. For a Christian is a compounded creature; he hath not only body and soul, but flesh and spirit. He is but in part renewed; and therefore, having in him both flesh and spirit, he is subject to hardness of heart; and it is clear that it may be so. Examples show that God's children are not always alike sensible of the wrath of God and of his mercy. They do not yield so to his commands as they should. But what is the reason that God doth suffer his children to fall into this hardness of heart? There is something in us that makes him give us up unto it, for we are no longer soft than he works upon us.

*Quest.* But what doth move him to leave us in this disposition?

*Sol.* I answer, he doth it for correction of former negligences, for sins of omission; especially when they neglect some means of grace whereby their hearts might be kept tender: it is for want of stirring up of God's grace in them; for want of an high esteem of grace bestowed upon them; want of care of their company, for not associating themselves with such as are tender-hearted; and from hence it comes that God suffers his children to fall into hardness of heart.

*Quest.* But now, from hence ariseth another question: How may a man know his heart from the heart of a reprobate, seeing that God's children may have hardness of heart?

*Ans.* I answer, that the heart of a man that is a very reprobate is totally, wholly, and finally hardened, and it is joined with security and insensibleness; it is joined with obstinacy, and with contempt of the means. But the child of God hath not total and final hardness of heart, but hath a sensibleness of it, he feeleth and seeth it. Total hardness doth feel nothing, but a Christian that hath hardness of heart, doth feel that he hath it; as a man that hath the stone in his bladder, feels and knows that he hath a stone. A hard-hearted man feels nothing, but he that hath but only hardness of heart doth feel: for there is difference between *hardness of heart* and a *hard heart;* for the child of God may have hardness of heart, but not a hard heart. Now, I say a child of God that hath hardness of heart is sensible of his hardness, and performs the actions of a sensible soul: he useth some good means for the softening of it, for the sense thereof is grievous to him above all other crosses; and whiles he is under it, he thinks that all is not with him as it should be: therefore he complains of it above all other afflictions, which makes him cry to God, as we may see, *Isa.* 63:17, 'Why hast thou hardened our hearts from thy fear?'

*Obj.* But some may demand how God doth harden.

*Sol.* I answer, the cause is first from our own selves; but he hardens four ways:

First, *Privatively,* by withholding and withdrawing his melting and softening power. For as the sun causeth darkness by withdrawing his light and warming power, so God withdrawing that melting power whereby we should be softened, it cannot be but that we must needs be hardened.

2. Secondly, *Negatively,* by denying of grace; by taking away from us his graces, which are not natural in us. Thus God doth to those whom he doth absolutely harden; he takes away that which they have, and so they become worse than they of themselves were by nature. When men walk unworthy of the gospel, God takes away very rational life from them, and gives them up to hardness of heart, that they run on in such courses, as that they are their own enemies, and bring upon themselves ruin.

3. Thirdly, And as God hardens by privation and negation, so, in the third place, he hardens by *tradition:*[6] by giving us up to the devil, to be vexed by his troubles, to harden us. It is a fearful judgment. When we take a course to grieve the Spirit of God, the Spirit will take a course to grieve us: he will give us up to Satan, to blind and to harden us. So that though God doth not work, as the author, effectually in this hardening, yet as a just judge he doth, by giving us up to Satan and the natural lusts of our own hearts, which are worse than all the devils in hell.

4. Fourthly and lastly, He doth harden *objectively,*

[6] That is, 'giving up'. Cf. *1 Tim.* 1:20 for the word.

by propounding good objects, which, meeting with a wicked heart, make it more hard, as, *Isa.* 6:10, it is said, 'Harden these people's hearts.' How? By preaching of the word. A good object, if it lights upon a bad soul, hardens the heart; for they that are not bettered by religion, under the means, are so much the worse by their use. So we see God cannot be impeached with the hardening of our hearts, because all the cause is from ourselves; for whether he hardens by privation, negation, tradition, or by propounding good objects, it is all from ourselves; and likewise we have seen that God's children may have hardness of heart in some measure, but yet it differs from a reprobate, because they see and feel it, grieve for it, and complain of it to God.

*Quest.* The second question is, *But whether may a child of God be more sensible of outward joys or crosses, than of spiritual things?* for this makes many think they have not tender hearts, because they are more sensible of outward things than of spiritual.

*Ans.* I answer, *It is not always alike with them;* for God's children are still complaining of something: of their carelessness in good duties, of their want of strength against corruption. They go mourning when they have made God to bring them down upon their knees for their hardness of heart; but there is an intercourse, in the children of God, between the flesh and the spirit. They are partly flesh and partly spirit. Therefore many times, for a while, when the flesh prevails, there may be a sudden joy and a sudden sorrow, which may be greater than spiritual joy or spiritual sorrow; but yet it is not continual. But spiritual sorrow, grief for sin, though it be not so vehement as, for the sudden, outward sorrow is, yet it is more constant. Grief for sin is continual; whereas outward sorrow is but upon a sudden, though it seem to be more violent.

2. And again, *in regard of their valuing and prizing of earthly things,* there may be a sudden sorrow: for a child of God may, upon a sudden, overprize outward things, and esteem them at too high a rate; but yet after that, valuing things by good advice, they prize spiritual things far beyond outward; and therefore their sorrow and joy is more for spiritual things, because it is constant. This I speak, not to cherish any neglect in any Christian, but for comfort to such as are troubled for it; therefore let such know, that God will not 'break the bruised reed, nor quench the smoking flax'. If they have but a desire, and by conscionable[7] use of means, do show their desire to be true, they shall have it at last, for Christ doth

---

[7] That is, 'conscientious'.

continue to make intercession for us, and if there were no weakness in us, what need Christ continue to make peace for us? for peace is made for those that fall out. Therefore, if there were no falling out between God and us, what need Christ to continue to make intercession for us? For these reasons, we see a child of God, for the present, may be more sensible of outward things than of spiritual.

*Quest.* But here another question may be asked, How shall we know that we have sensibleness and pliableness, or not?

*Ans.* I answer, Easily, by applying of the soul unto objects, as 1, to God; 2, to his word; 3, to his works; 4, to man.

We may try our tenderness and pliableness of heart these four ways:

1. *To God.* As it is tender *from* God, so it is tender *for* God; for the three persons of the Trinity. He that hath a tender heart cannot endure to dishonour God himself, or to hear others dishonour him, either by his own sins or by others'. He cannot endure to hear God's name blasphemed. So that they have a tender heart who, when they see Christ in his religion to be wronged, cannot choose but be affected with it. So again, a man hath a tender heart when he yields to the motions of the Holy Ghost. When

the Spirit moves, and he yields, this shows there is a tender heart. But a hard heart beats back all, and as a stone to the hammer, will not yield to any motion of God's Spirit.

2. Now, in the second place, to come downward, a tender heart is sensible in regard of *the word of God*; as, first, at the threatenings a true tender heart will tremble, as *Isa.* 66:2, 'To him will I look, even to him that is of a contrite and broken spirit, and trembleth at my words.' A man that hath a tender heart will tremble at the signs of the anger of God: 'Shall the lion roar, and the beasts of the forest not be afraid?' (*Amos* 3:4). Yes, they will stand still and tremble at the roaring of the lion; but much more will a tender heart tremble when God roars, and threatens vengeance. A tender heart will tremble when it hears of the terrors of the Lord at the day of judgment, as Paul did: 'Now knowing the terrors of the Lord, we persuade men' (2 *Cor.* 5:11). It forced him to be faithful in his office. This use the apostle Peter would have us make of it: 'That seeing all these things must be dissolved, what manner of persons ought we to be in holy conversation and godliness?' (2 *Pet.* 3:11). And so for the promises in the word. The heart is tender when the word of God doth rejoice a man above all things. How can the heart but melt at God's promises,

for they are the sweetest things that can be. Therefore when a tender heart hears God's promises, it makes him to melt and be sensible of them. Again, a tender heart will be pliable to any direction in the word. To God's call it will answer, 'Here I am; Lord, what wilt thou have me to do?' As Isaiah, when he had once a tender heart, then 'Send me, Lord' (*Isa.* 6:8). So David to God's command, 'Seek ye my face', answers, 'Thy face, Lord, will I seek' (*Psa.* 27:8). There is a gracious echo of the soul to God in whatsoever he saith in his word. And thus a true, tender heart doth yield to the word of God, and is fit to run on any errand.

3. Thirdly, By applying it *to the works of God;* for a tender heart quakes when it doth see the judgment of God abroad upon others. It hastens to make its peace with God, and to meet him by repentance. So again, a tender heart rejoiceth at the mercy of God, for it doth see something in it better than the thing itself; and that is the love of God, from which it doth proceed.

4. Fourthly, A man may know his heart to be tender and sensible, in regard of *the estate of others, whether they be good or bad.* If they be wicked, he hath a tender heart for them; as David (*Psa.* 119:136), 'Mine eyes gush out with rivers of water, because men keep not thy law.' So Paul saith, 'There are many that walk inordinately, of whom I have told you before,

and now tell you weeping, *etc.*' (*Phil.* 3:18). So Christ was sensible of the misery of Jerusalem, wept for it, and a little while after, shed his own blood for it (*Matt.* 23:37, *Luke* 19:41–44). Thus had he a tender heart. But when Christ looked to God's decree, he saith, 'Father, I thank thee, Lord of heaven and earth, that thou hast hid these things from the wise and noble, and hast revealed them unto babes' (*Matt.* 11:25). And so likewise for those that are good, in giving and forgiving; in giving, they give not only the thing, but they give their hearts and affections with it; and so in forgiving, they apprehend Christ's love in forgiving them; therefore they forgive others. So for works, will God have a tender heart to do anything, it will do it. If he will have it mourn, it will mourn; if to rejoice, it will rejoice; it is fit for every good work. By these marks we may know whether we have tender hearts or no.

But to apply this; how is this affection of Josiah in the hearts of men in these days? How many have melting hearts when they hear God blasphemed, and the religion of Christ wronged? How few are there that yield to the motions of the Spirit! We may take up a wonderful complaint of the hardness of men's hearts in these days, who never tremble at the word of God. Neither his promises, nor threatenings, nor commands will melt their hearts; but this is certain, that they which are not better under religion, by the means of grace, are much the worse. And how sensible are we of the church's miseries? For a tender heart is sensible of the miseries of the church, as being members of the same body, whereof Christ is the head. But men nowadays are so far from melting hearts, that they want natural affection, as Paul foretells of such in the latter times (*1 Tim.* 4:1). They have less bowels of pity in them, when they hear how it goes with the church abroad, than very pagans and heathens. This shews they have no tender hearts, that they are not knit to Christ by faith, who is the head; nor to the church, the body, in love. How is thy heart affected to men when they commit any sin against God, as idolaters, swearers, drunkards, liars, and the like? Is it mercy to let these go on in their sins towards hell? No, this is cruelty; but mercy is to be showed unto them, in restraining men from their wicked courses. Therefore do not think thou showest mercy unto them by letting them alone in sin, but exhort and instruct them. Coldness and deadness is a spiritual disease in these days. But surely they that have the Spirit of God warming their hearts, are sensible of their own good and ill, and of the good and ill of the time. Well, if you will know you have a tender heart, look to God, look to his word, to his works, to yourselves, and others; and so you shall know whether you have tender hearts or not.

*Quest.* But here may be another question asked, How shall men recover themselves, when they are subject to this hardness, deadness, and insensibleness? If after examination a man find himself to be thus, how shall he recover himself out of this estate? I answer,

*Ans.* 1. First, As when things are cold we bring them to the fire to heat and melt, *so bring we our cold hearts to the fire of the love of Christ;* consider we of our sins against Christ, and of Christ's love towards us; dwell upon this meditation. Think what great love Christ hath showed unto us, and how little we have deserved, and this will make our hearts to melt and be as pliable as wax before the sun.

2. Secondly, If thou wilt have this tender and melting heart, then *use the means;* be always under the sunshine of the gospel. Be under God's sunshine, that he may melt thy heart; be constant in good means; and help one another. 'We must provoke one another daily, lest any be hardened through the deceitfulness of sin' (*Heb.* 3:13). Physicians love not to give physic[8] to themselves. So a man is not always fit to help

---

[8] That is, 'medicine'.

himself when he is not right, but good company is fit to do it. 'Did not our hearts burn within us while he talked with us?' said the two disciples, holding communion each with other at Emmaus (*Luke* 24:32). For then Christ comes and makes a third, joins with them, and so makes their hearts burn within them. So Christ saith, 'Where two or three are met together in his name, he is in the midst of them' (*Matt.* 18:20). Now they were under the promise, therefore he affords his presence. Where two hold communion together, there Christ will make a third. Therefore let us use the help of others, seeing David could not recover himself, being a prophet, but he must have a Nathan to help him (2 *Sam.* 12:7). Therefore if we would recover ourselves from hard and insensible hearts, let us use the help one of another.

3. Thirdly, *We must with boldness and reverence challenge the covenant of grace;* for this is the covenant that God hath made with us, to give us tender hearts, hearts of flesh (as *Ezek.* 11:19, 'I will give them one heart, find put a new spirit within their bowels; I will take away the stony hearts out of their bodies, and I will give them a heart of flesh'). Now seeing this is a covenant God hath made, to give us fleshly hearts and to take away our stony, let us challenge him with his promise, and go to him by

prayer. Entreat him to give thee a fleshly heart; go to him, wait his time, for that is the best time. Therefore wait though he do not hear at first. These are the means to bring tenderness of heart.

Now, that ye may be stirred up to this duty, namely, to get a soft and tender heart, mark here,

1. First, *What an excellent thing a tender heart is.* God hath promised to dwell in such an heart, and it is an excellent thing to have God dwell in our hearts, as he hath promised: 'For thus saith he that is high and excellent, he that inhabiteth eternity, whose name is the Holy One: I will dwell in the high and holy place, and with him also that is of a contrite and humble spirit, to revive the spirit of the humble, and to give life to them that are of a contrite heart?' (*Isa.* 57:15), So *Isa.* 66:2, 'To him will I look, even to him that is poor and contrite in spirit, and doth tremble at my words.' Now God having promised to dwell where there is a soft heart, and no hardness, no rocks to keep him out; can God come into a heart without a blessing? Can he be separated from goodness, which is goodness itself? When the heart therefore is pliable and thus tender, there is an immediate communion between the soul and God; and can that heart be miserable that hath communion with God? Surely no.

2. Secondly, *Consider that this doth fit a man for the end for which he was created*. A man is never fit for that end for which he was made, but when he hath a tender heart; and what are we redeemed for, but that we should serve God? And who is fit to be put in the service of God but he that hath begged a tender heart of God?

3. Thirdly, To stir you up to labour for this, *consider that a tender heart is fit for any blessedness*. It is capable of any beatitude. What makes a man blessed in anything but a tender heart? This will make a man to hear the word, to read, to show mercies to others. 'Blessed are the poor in spirit', saith Christ, 'for theirs is the kingdom of heaven.' A tender heart is blessed, because that only heareth God's word, and doth it; and it is always a merciful heart, and therefore blessed.

4. Again, *Consider the wretched estate of a heart contrary, that is not tender, and will not yield*. Oh what a wonderful hardness would the heart of man grow to, if we do not follow it with means to soften it! What a fearful thing was it to see what strange things fell out at Christ's death, what darkness there was, what thunders and lightnings. The veil of the temple rent, the sun was turned into darkness, the graves opened, and the dead did rise, yet notwithstanding

none of these would make the hypocritical Pharisees to tremble, but they mocked at it, although it made a very heathen man confess it the work of God (*Matt.* 27:45-54). For a ceremonial hypocrite is more hard than a Turk, Jew, or Pagan. All the judgments of God upon Pharaoh were not so great as hardness of heart. The papists, after they have been at their superstitious devotion, are fittest for powderplots and treasons,[9] because their hearts are so much more hardened. What fearful things may a man come to, if he give way to hardness of heart! He may come to an estate like the devil, yea, worse than Judas, for he had some sensibleness of his sin; he confessed he had sinned in betraying the innocent blood. But many of these hypocrites have no sensibleness at all, which is a fearful thing. Eli's children hearkened not to the voice of their father, because that the Lord had a purpose to destroy them (*1 Sam.* 2:25). So it is in this case a shrewd sign that God will destroy those that are so insensible that nothing will work upon them. But these hypocrites shall be sensible one day, when they shall wish they were as insensible as in

[9]An allusion to the the Gunpowder Plot of 1605, in earlier centuries often called the Gunpowder Treason Plot, which was a failed assassination attempt against King James I of England (James VI of Scotland) by a group of provincial English Roman Catholics which included the infamous Guy Fawkes.

their lifetime they were. But it will be an unfruitful repentance to repent in hell; for there a man shall get no benefit by his repentance, seeing *there* they cannot shake off the execution of God's judgment, as they shake off the threatenings of his judgments *here*. Well, to this fearful end, before it be long, must everyone that hath a hard heart come, unless they repent. Therefore let everyone be persuaded to labour for a tender, pliable, yielding, and sensible heart here, else we shall have it hereafter against our wills when it will do us no good; for then hypocrites shall be sensible against their wills, though they would not be sensible in this life.

And thus I have done with the first inward cause in Josiah that moved God so to respect him, namely, tenderness of heart.

# 2

---

# THE ART OF
# SELF-HUMBLING

*Because thine heart was tender, and thou didst
humble thyself before God, when thou heardest his
words against this place, and against the inhabitants
thereof, and humbledst thyself before me, and didst
rend thy clothes, and weep before me, etc.*

2 Chron. 34:27

OF tenderness of heart, the first inward cause in
Josiah, which moved God to pity him, so as he
should not be an eye-witness of the fearful calamities
to come upon his land and people, is largely spoken
in the former sermon: wherein is also showed how
it is wrought, preserved, discerned, recovered when
it is lost; what encouragements we have to seek and
labour for it, with some other things which I will

not here repeat, but fall directly upon that which follows, 'And thou didst humble thyself before God.' In which words we have set down the second inward cause in Josiah, that moved God to show mercy unto him; the humbling of himself. 'And thou didst humble thyself before God.' Tenderness of heart and humbling a man's self go both together; for things that are hard will not yield nor bow. A great iron bar will not bow, a hard stony heart will not yield. Now, therefore, humbling of ourselves, the making of us as low as the ground itself, is added unto tenderness; for the soul being once tender and melting, is fit to be humbled, yea, cares not how low it be abased, so mercy may follow. For the better unfolding of the words, we will consider,

1. *The person that did humble himself:* 'Josiah', a king, a great man.

2. *Humiliation itself, and the qualities of it:* 'and humbledst thyself before God', which argued the sincerity of it.

3. *The occasion of it:* 'when thou heardest the words against this place, and against the inhabitants thereof.'

4. *The outward expression of it, in weeping and rending his clothes;* which we will handle in their place.

1. First, for the *person*, 'Thou didst humble thyself', Josiah a king, who was tenderly brought up, and highly advanced; a thing which makes the work so much the more commendable; whence we learn,

Doct. 1. *That it is a disposition not unbefitting kings to humble themselves before God*. For howsoever they are gods downward, to those that are under them, yet if they look upward, what are kings? The greater light hides the lesser. What are all the inhabitants of the earth in his sight but as a drop of a bucket, as dust upon the balance, of no moment! (*Isa.* 40:15). 'I have said you are gods, but you shall die like men' (*Psa.* 82:6-7). For howsoever the saints of God differ from other men in regard of their use, and the inscription God hath set upon them, yet they are of the same stuff, dust, as others are. And so kings, though in civil respects they differ from other men, yet are they of the same metal, and shall end in death, all their glory must lie in the dust.

Therefore it is not unbefitting kings to humble themselves before God, seeing they have to deal with him who is a 'consuming fire' (*Heb.* 12:29), before whom the very angels cover their faces. I say it is no shame for the greatest monarch of the earth to abase himself when he hath to do with God; yea, kings, of all other persons, ought most to humble themselves, to show their thankfulness to God, who hath raised them from their brethren to be heads of his people. And considering the endowments which kings usually have, they are bound to humble themselves, as also in regard of the authority and power which God hath put into their hands, saying, 'By me kings reign' (*Prov.* 8:15). But usually we see, from the beginning of the world, that kings forget God. Where there is not grace above nature, there kings will not stoop to Christ; but so far as it agrees with their pleasure and will, so far shall Christ be served, and no farther.

But yet God hath always raised up some nursing fathers and mothers—as he hath done to us, for which we ought to bless God—who have and do make conscience of this mentioned duty, so well beseeming Christian princes, as in sundry other respects, so also in this, that therein they might be exemplary to the people. For no doubt but Josiah did this also, that his people might not think it a shame for them to humble themselves before God, whenas he their king, tender in years, and subject to no earthly man, did before them, in his own person, prostrate himself in the humblest manner before the great God of heaven and earth.

As that ointment poured upon Aaron's head fell from his head to the skirt—and so spread itself to the rest of the parts, even to his feet (*Psa.* 133:2), so a good example in a king descends down to the lowest subjects, as the rain from the mountains to the valleys. Therefore a king should first begin to humble himself. Kings are called fathers to their subjects, because they should bear a loving and holy affection to their people, that when anything troubles the subjects, they should be affected with it. Governors are not to have a distinct good from their subjects, but the welfare of the subjects should be the glory of their head. Therefore Josiah took the judgments threatened as his own: howsoever his estate was nothing unto theirs.

It is said moreover, 'Thou didst humble thyself.' He was both the agent and the patient, the worker and the object of his work: it came from him, and ended in him. Humiliation is a reflected action: Josiah humbled himself. And certainly this is that true humiliation, the humbling of ourselves; for it is no thanks for a man to be humbled by God, as Pharaoh was; for God can humble and pull down the proudest that do oppose his church. God by this gets himself glory. But here is the glory of a Christian, that he hath got grace from God to humble himself; which humbling is, from our own judgment, and upon discerning of good grounds, to bring our affections to stoop unto God; to humble ourselves. Many are humbled that are not humble; many are cast down that have proud hearts still, as Pharaoh had. It is said, 'Thou humbledst thyself.' Then we learn,

Doct. 2. *That the actions of grace are reflected actions.* They begin from a man's self and end in a man's self; yet we must not exclude the Spirit of God; for he doth not say, thou from thyself didst humble thyself, but 'thou didst humble thyself.' We have grace from God to humble ourselves. So that the Spirit of God doth work upon us as upon fit subjects, in which grace doth work. Though such works be the works of God, yet they are said to be ours, because God doth work them in us and by us. We are said to humble ourselves, because we are temples wherein he works, seeing he useth the parts of our soul, as the understanding, the will, and the affections, in the work. Therefore it is foolish for the papists to say, good works be our own, as from ourselves. No; good works, say we, are ours, as effects of the Spirit in us. But for the further expression of this humbling of ourselves before God, we will consider,

1. The kinds and degrees of it.

2. Some directions how we may humble ourselves.

3. The motives to move us to it.

4. The notes whereby it may be known.

1. First, for the *nature and kinds of it;* we must know that humiliation is either

(1.) *Inward, in the mind* first of all, and then in the *affections;* or,

(2.) *Outward , in expression of words,* and likewise in *carriage.*

(1.) To begin with the first, *inward humiliation in the mind,* in regard of judgment and knowledge, is, *when our understandings are convinced, that we are as we are;* when we are not high-minded, but when we judge meanly and basely of ourselves, both in regard of our beginning and dependency upon God, having all from him, both life, motion, and being; and also in regard of our end, what we shall be ere long. All glory shall end in the dust, all honouring in the grave, and all riches in poverty. And withal, true humiliation is also in regard of spiritual respects, when we judge aright how base and vile we are in regard of our natural corruption, that we are by nature not only guilty of Adam's sin, but that we have, besides that, wrapt ourselves in a thousand more guilts by our sinful course of life, and that we have nothing of our own, no, not power to do the least good thing. When we look upon any vile person, we may see our own image. So that if God had not been gracious unto us, we should have been as bad as they. In a word, inward conviction of our natural frailty and misery, in regard of the filthy and foul stain of sin in our nature and actions, and of the many guilts of spiritual and temporal plagues in this life and that which is to come, is that inward humiliation in the judgment or understanding.

Again, Inward humiliation, besides spiritual conviction, is *when there are affections of humiliation.* And what be those? Shame, sorrow, fear, and such like penal afflictive affections. For, upon a right conviction of the understanding, the soul comes to be stricken with shame that we are in such a case as we are; especially when we consider God's goodness to us, and our dealing with him. This will breed shame and abasement, as it did in Daniel. Shame and sorrow ever follow sin, first or last, as the apostle demands (*Rom.* 6:21), 'What fruit had ye then in those things whereof ye are now ashamed?' After conviction of judgment there is always shame; and likewise there is sorrow and grief. For God hath made the inward faculties of the soul so, that upon the apprehension of the understanding, the heart comes to be stricken through with grief, which works upon our souls. Therefore we are said in Scripture to afflict ourselves;

that is, when we set ourselves upon meditation of our deserts. Hereupon we cannot but be affected inwardly, for these sorrows are so many daggers to pierce through the heart.

The third penal affection is, *fear and trembling before God's judgments and his threatenings,* a fear of the majesty of God, whom we have offended, which is able to send us to hell if his mercies were not beyond our deserts. But his mercy it is, that we are not consumed. A fear of this great God is a part of this inward humiliation. So we see what inward humiliation is: first, a conviction of the judgment; and then it proceeds to inward afflictive affections, as grief, shame, fear, which, when upon good ground and fit objects, they are wrought in us by the Holy Ghost, they are parts of inward humiliation. But as for the wicked, they drown themselves in their profaneness, because they would not be ashamed, nor fear, nor grieve for them. But this makes way for terrible shame, sorrow, and fear afterwards; for those that will not shame, grieve, and fear here, shall be ashamed before God and his angels at the day of judgment, and shall be tormented in hell for ever.

2. Secondly, His *outward humiliation* is expressed and manifested in words, in outward behaviour and carriage. The words which he used are not here set

down; but certainly Josiah did speak words when he humbled himself. It was not a dumb show, but done with his outward expression and his inward affection. This is evident by those words of the text, 'I have heard thee also', saith the Lord. Without doubt, therefore, he did speak something. But because true sorrow cannot speak distinctly—for a broken soul can speak but broken words—therefore his words are not here set down, but yet God heard them well enough. And indeed, so it is sometimes, that the grief for the affliction may be stronger than the faculty of speech, so that a man cannot speak for grief. As a heathen man, by light of nature, did weep and grieve for his friends, but when his child came to be killed before him, he stood like a stone, because his sorrow was so great that it exceeded all expression. So humiliation may so exceed that it cannot be expressed in words; as David himself, when he was told of his sins by Nathan, did not express all his sorrow, but saith, 'I have sinned'; yet afterwards, he makes the 51st Psalm, a composed speech for supply, a fit pattern for an humble and broken soul. So doubtless there was outward expression of words in Josiah, although they be not here set down. This speech, which is a part of humiliation, is called a confession of our sins to God; with it should be joined hatred and grief afflictive, as also a deprecation and desire that God would remove the judgment which we have deserved by our sins; and likewise a justification of God, in what he hath laid, or may lay, upon us. Lord, thou art righteous and just in all thy judgments; shame and confusion belongeth unto me; my sins have deserved that thou shouldest pour down thy vengeance upon me; it is thy great mercy that I am not consumed. The good thief upon the cross justified God, saying, 'We are here justly for our deserts; but this man doth suffer wrongfully' (*Luke* 23:41). Justification and self-condemnation go with humiliation. This is the outward expression in words. Now the outward humiliation in respect of his carriage, is here directly set down in two acts: 1. *Rending of clothes*. And 2. *Weeping*. But of these I shall speak afterwards when I come at them. Thus we have seen the degrees and kinds of humiliation.

Seeing it is such a necessary qualification, for humiliation is a fundamental grace that gives strength to all other graces; seeing, I say, it is such a necessary temper of a holy gracious man to be humble; how may we come to humble ourselves as we should do? I answer, Let us take these directions:

1. First, *Get poor spirits,* that is, spirits to see the wants in ourselves and in the creature; the emptiness

of all earthly things without God's favour; the insul-ficiency of ourselves and of the creature at the day of judgment; for what the wise man saith of riches may be truly said of all other things under the sun: they avail not in the day of wrath, but righteousness delivereth from death (*Prov.* 11:4).

Josiah was not poor in respect of the world, for he was a king; but he was 'poor in spirit', because he saw an emptiness in himself. He knew his kingdom could not shield him from God's judgment, if he were once angry.

(1.) Let us consider our *original*. From whence came we? From the earth, from nothing. Whither go we? To the earth, to nothing. And in respect of spiritual things, we have nothing. We are not able to do anything of ourselves, no, not so much as to think a good thought.

(2.) Likewise, consider we *the guilt of our sins*. What do we deserve? Hell and damnation, to have our portion with hypocrites in that 'lake that burneth with fire and brimstone'.

(3.) Let us have before our eyes the picture of old Adam, our sinful nature: how we are drawn away by every object; how ready to be proud of anything; how unable to resist the least sin; how ready to be cast down under every affliction; that we cannot rejoice in any blesssing; that we have no strength of ourselves to perform any good or suffer ill; in a word, how that we carry a nature about us indisposed to good, and prone to all evil. This consideration humbled Paul, and made him to cry out, when no other afflictions could move him, 'O miserable man that I am, who shall deliver me from this body of death?' (*Rom.* 7:24). By this means we come to be poor in spirit.

2. If we would have humble spirits, let us *bring ourselves into the presence of the great God*: set ourselves in his presence, and consider of his attributes, his works of justice abroad in the world, and open[1] ourselves in particular.

Consider his wisdom, holiness, power, and strength, with our own. It will make us abhor ourselves, and repent in dust and ashes. Let us bring ourselves into God's presence, be under the means, under his word, that there we may see ourselves ripped up, and see what we are. As Job, when he brought himself into God's presence, said, 'I abhor myself, and repent in dust and ashes' (*Job* 42:6). Job thought himself somebody before; but when God comes to examine him, and upon examination found that he could not give a reason of the creature, much less of the Lord's afflicting his children, then

---

[1] Should this read 'upon'? — *Ed.*

he saith, 'I abhor myself.' So Abraham, the more he talked with God, the more he did see himself but dust and ashes. This is the language of the holy men in Scripture, when they have to deal or think of God. 'I am not worthy', says John Baptist (*John* 1:27). So Paul: 'I am not worthy to be called an apostle' (*1 Cor.* 15:9). So the centurion: 'I am not worthy thou shouldst come into my house' (*Matt.* 8:8). 'I am less than the least of thy blessings', saith Jacob (*Gen.* 32:10). Thus let us come into the presence of God, under the means of his word, and then we shall see our own vileness, which will work humiliation; for, as the apostle saith, when a poor simple man doth come, and hears the prophecy, that is, the word of God, with application unto himself, laying open his particular sins, doubtless he will say, God is in you (*1 Cor.* 14:24-25).

3. That we may humble ourselves, *let us be content to hear of our sins and baseness by others*. Let us be content that others should acquaint us with anything that may humble us. Proud men are the devil's pipes, and flatterers the musicians to blow these pipes. Therefore it is, that though men have nothing of their own, yet they love to give heed to flatterers, to blow their bladder full, which do rob them of themselves; whereas a true, wise man, will

be content to hear of anything that may humble him before God.

4. And withal, that we may humble ourselves, *look to the time to come, what we shall be ere long,* earth and dust; and at the day of judgment we must be stripped of all. What should puff us up in this world? All our glory shall end in shame, all magnificency in confusion, all riches in poverty. It is a strange thing that the devil should raise men to be proud of that which they have not of their own, but of such things which they have borrowed and begged; as for men to be proud of themselves in regard of their parents. So, many there are who think the better of themselves for their apparel, when yet they are clothed with nothing of their own, and so are proud of the very creature. But thus the devil hath besotted our nature, to make us glory in that which should abase us, and to think the better of ourselves, for that which is none of our own. Nay, many in the church of God are so far from humbling themselves, that they come to manifest their pride, to show themselves, to see and to be seen. Thus the devil besots many thousand silly creatures, that come in vainglory into the house of God; that whereas they should humble themselves before him, they are puffed up with a base empty pride, even before God. Therefore let us take notice of our

wonderful proneness to have a conceit of ourselves; for if a man have a new fashion, or some new thing, which nobody else knows besides himself, how wonderful conceited will he be of himself!

Let us take notice, I say, of our proneness to this sin of pride; for the best are prone to it. Consider, it is a wonderful hateful sin, a sin of sins, that God most hates. It was this sin that made him thrust Adam out of paradise. It was this sin which made him thrust the evil angels out of heaven, who shall never come there again. Yea, it is a sin that God cures with other sins, so far he hateth it; as Paul, being subject to be proud through the abundance of revelations, was cured of it by a prick in the flesh: being exercised with some dangerous, noisome, and strange cure. Indeed, it is profitable for some men to fall, that so by their humiliation for infirmities, they may be cured of this great, this sacrilegious sin. And why is it called a sacrilegious sin? Because it robs God of his glory. For God hath said, 'My glory I will not give to another' (*Isa.* 42:8). Is not the grace, goodness, and mercy of God sufficient for us, but we must enter into his prerogatives, and exalt ourselves? We are both idols and idol-worshippers, when we think highly of ourselves, for we make ourselves idols. Now God hates idolatry; but pride is a sacrilege, therefore God hates pride.

5. If we would humble ourselves, *let us set before us the example of our blessed Saviour;* for we must be conformable to him, by whom we hope to be saved. He left heaven, took our base nature, and humbled himself to the death of the cross, yea, to the washing of his disciples' feet, and among the rest, washed Judas's feet, and so suffered himself to be killed as a traitor (*Phil.* 2:5-8); and all this to satisfy the wrath of God for us, and that he might be a pattern for us to be like-minded. Therefore, if we would humble ourselves by pattern, here is a pattern without all exception. Let us be transformed into the likeness of him; yea, the more we think of him, the more we shall be humbled. For it is impossible for a man to dwell upon this meditation of Christ in humility, and with faith to apply it to himself, that he is his particular Saviour, but this faith will abase the heart, and bring it to be like Christ in all spiritual representation. A heart that believeth in Christ will be humbled like Christ. It will be turned from all fleshly conceit of excellency, to be like him. Is it possible, if a man consider he is to be saved by an abased and humble Saviour, that was pliable to every base service, that had not a house to hide himself; I say, is it possible that he which considers of this, should ever be willingly or wilfully proud? Do we hope to be saved by Christ, and will we

not be like him? When we were firebrands of hell, he humbled himself to the death of the cross, left heaven and happiness awhile, and took our shame, to be a pattern to us. We know that Christ was brought into the world by an humble virgin. So the heart wherein he dwells must be an humble heart. If we have true faith in Christ, it will cast us down, and make us to be humbled. For it is impossible that a man should have faith to challenge any part in Christ, except he be conformed to the image of Christ in humility. Therefore let us take counsel of Christ: 'Learn of me, for I am humble and meek; and so you shall find rest to your souls' (*Matt.* 11:29).

Lastly, That we may humble ourselves, *let us work upon our own souls by reasoning, discoursing, and speaking to our own hearts*. For the soul hath a faculty to work upon itself. Now this, being a reflected action, to humble ourselves, it must be done by some inward action; and what is that? To discourse thus: 'If so be a prince should but frown upon me when I have offended his law, in what case should I be! Yet, when the great God of heaven threatens, what an atheistical unbelieving heart have I, that can be moved at the threatenings of a mortal man, that is but dust and ashes, and yet cannot be moved with the threatenings of the great God!' Consider also:

'If a man had been so kind and bountiful to me, if I should reward his kindness with unkindness, I should have been ashamed, and have covered my face with shame; and yet how unkind have I been unto God that hath been so kind to me, and yet I never a whit ashamed! If a friend should have come to me, and I have given him no entertainment, what a shame were this! But yet how often hath the Holy Ghost knocked at the door of my heart, and suggested many holy motions into me of mortification, repentance, and newness of life, yet notwithstanding I have given him the repulse, opposed the outward means of grace, and have thought myself unworthy of it; what a shame is this!'

Thus, if we compare our carriage in earthly things with our carriage in heavenly, this will be a means to work upon our hearts, inwardly to humble ourselves. Thus was David abased; for when Nathan came and told him of a rich man, who having many sheep, spared his own and took away a poor man's, which was all that he had; when David considered that he had so dealt with Uriah, he was dejected and ashamed of his own courses. Let us labour to work our hearts to humility, into true sorrow, shame, true fear, that so we may have God to pity and respect us, who only doth regard an humble soul. Thus we have seen some directions how we may come to humble ourselves.

Further, there is an order, method, and agreement in these reflected actions, when we turn the edge of our own souls upon ourselves and examine ourselves; for the way that leads to rest is by the examination of ourselves. We must examine ourselves strictly, and then bring ourselves before God, judge and condemn ourselves; for humiliation is a kind of execution. Examination leads to all the rest. So, then, this is the order of our actions; there is examination of ourselves strictly before God, then indicting ourselves, after that comes judging of ourselves.

Oh that we could be brought to these inward reflected actions, to examine indict, judge, and condemn ourselves, that so we might spare God a labour, and so all things might go well with us!

3. Now. I come to the third thing I propounded, *the motives to move us to get this humiliation.*

(1.) First, *Let us consider of the gracious promises that are made to this disposition of humbling ourselves;* as *Isa.* 57:15: 'For thus saith he that is holy and excellent, he that inhabiteth eternity, whose name is the Holy One; I dwell in the high and holy place, with him also that is of an humble and contrite spirit, to revive the spirit of the humble, and to give life to them that are of a contrite heart.' So there is a promise that God will give grace to the humble. An example of mercy in this kind we have in Manasseh, who, though a very wicked man, yet because he humbled himself, obtained mercy. Peter humbled himself, and David humbled himself, and both found mercy. And so likewise Josiah; yea, and in James 4:10, we are bid to 'humble ourselves under the mighty hand of God, and he will exalt us in due time.' There is the promise. Yea, every branch of humiliation hath a promise. As confession of sins, if we confess and forsake our sins, we shall have mercy and find pardon. So those that judge themselves shall not be judged.

An humble heart is a vessel of all graces. It is a grace itself, and a vessel of grace. It doth better the soul and make it holy, for the soul is never fitter for God than when it is humbled. It is a fundamental grace that gives strength to all other graces. So much humility, so much grace. For according to the measure of humiliation is the measure of other grace, because an humble heart hath in it a spiritual emptiness. Humility emptieth the heart for God to fill it. If the heart be emptied of temporal things, then it must needs be filled with spiritual things; for nature abhorreth emptiness; grace much more. When the heart is made low, there is a spiritual emptiness, and what fills this up but the Spirit of God? In that measure we empty ourselves, in that measure we are filled with the fulness of God. When a man is humbled, he is fit for all good; but when he is proud, he is fit for all ill, and beats back all good. God hath but two heavens to dwell in; the heaven of heavens, and the heart of a poor humble man. The proud swelling heart, that is full of ambition, high conceits, and self-dependence, will not endure to have God to enter; but he dwells largely and easily in the heart of an humble man. If we will dwell in heaven hereafter, let us humble ourselves now. The rich in themselves are sent 'empty away'; the humble soul is a rich soul, rich in God; and therefore God regards the lowly and resists the proud. As all the water that is upon the hills runs into the valleys, so all grace goes to the humble. 'The mountains of Gilboa are accursed' (2 *Sam.* 1:21). So there is a curse upon pride, because it will not yield to God.

(2.) Again, *All outward actions benefit other men; but this inward action of humbling a man's self makes the soul itself good.*

(3.) *An humble soul is a secure and safe soul;* for a man that is not high, but of a low stature, needs not to fear falling. An humble soul is a safe soul—safe in regard of outward troubles; for when we have humbled ourselves, God needs not follow us with any other judgment: safe, in regard of inward vexation or any trouble by God; for when the soul hath brought itself low, and laid itself level as the ground, then God ceaseth to afflict it. Will the ploughman plough when he hath broken up the ground enough? or doth he delight in breaking up the ground? See what Isaiah saith to this purpose in chapter 28:28. When God seeth that a man hath abased himself, he will not follow with any other judgment; such an one may say to God, 'Lord, I have kept court in mine own conscience already, I have humbled and judged myself, therefore do not thou judge me; I am ready to do whatsoever thou wilt, and to suffer what thou wilt have me. I have deserved worse a thousand times, but, Lord, remember I am but dust and ashes.' Thus God spares his labour when the soul hath humbled itself. But if we do not do this ourselves, God will take us in hand; for God will have but one God. Now if we will be gods, to exalt ourselves, he must take us in hand to humble us, either first or last. And is it not better for us to humble ourselves than for God to give us up to the merciless rage and fury of men, for them to humble us, or to fall into the hands of God who is a 'consuming fire'? For when we accuse and judge ourselves, we prevent much shame and sorrow. What is the reason God hath given us up to shame and crosses in this world, but because we have not humbled ourselves? What is the reason many are damned in hell? Because God hath given them reason, judgment, and affections, but they have not used them for themselves to examine their ways, whether they were in the state of condemnation or salvation. They never used their affections and judgment to this end, therefore God was forced to take them in hand. Well saith Augustine, all men must be humbled one way or other; either we must humble ourselves or God will;[2] if we will do this ourselves, the apostle promiseth, we shall not be judged of the Lord (*1 Cor.* 11:31). But we do not these things as we should, because it is a secret action. We love to do things that the world may take notice of, but this inward humiliation can only be seen by God, and by our own consciences. Let these motives therefore stir us up to humble ourselves, for humbled we must be, by one way or other. How many judgments might be avoided by humbling ourselves! How many scandals might be prevented if we would judge ourselves! What is the reason so many Christians fall into scandalous sins, whereby, provoking God's anger, they fall into the hands of their enemies, but because they

---

[2] In *Confessions* repeatedly.

spare themselves, and think this humbling themselves a troublesome action. Therefore to spare themselves, they run on. Because they would not work this upon themselves, they grow to be in a desperate state at last. Wherefore upon any occasion be humble, let us prepare ourselves to meet the Lord our God. When we hear but any noise of the judgments of God, we should humble ourselves, as good Josiah did; when he did but hear of the threatenings against his land, it made him humble himself.

*Quest.* But here it may be demanded, considering that wicked men do oftentimes humble themselves, being convinced in their consciences, and thereupon ashamed,

4. *How may we know holy from hypocritical humiliation?* which is the last thing I propounded concerning humiliation, namely, the notes and marks whereby we may know true humiliation from false, which are these.

*Ans.* 1. First, *Holy humiliation is voluntary;* for it is a reflected action, which comes from a man's self. It ends where it begins. Therefore Josiah is said to humble himself. But, on the contrary, the humiliation of other men is against their will. False humiliation is not voluntary, but by force it is extorted from them. God is fain to break, crush, and deal hardly with them, which they grieve and murmur at. But the children of God have the Spirit of God, which is a free Spirit, that sets their hearts at liberty. For God's Spirit is a working Spirit, that works upon their hearts, and hereby they willingly humble themselves, whereas the wicked, wanting this Spirit of God, cannot humble themselves willingly, but are cast down against their wills. For God can pluck down the proudest. He can break Pharaoh's courage, who, though he was humbled, yet he did not humble himself. A man may be *humbled,* and yet not *humble.* But the children of God are to humble themselves, not that the grace whereby we humble ourselves is from ourselves; but we are said to humble ourselves, when God doth rule the parts he hath given us, when he sets our wits and understanding on work to see our misery, and then our will and affection to work upon these. Thus we are said to humble ourselves when God works in us. An hypocrite God may humble and work by him. He may work by graceless persons, but he doth not work in them. But God's children have God's Spirit in them, not only working in[3] them his own works, as he doth by hypocrites and sinful persons, but his Spirit works in them. So that here is the main difference between true humiliation and that which is

[3] Should this read 'by'? — *Ed.*

counterfeit. The one is voluntary, being a reflected action, to work upon and to humble ourselves; but the other is a forced humiliation.

2. Again, *True humiliation is ever joined with reformation*. Humble thyself and walk with thy God, saith the prophet: 'He hath showed thee, O man, what he doth require of thee, to humble thyself, and walk with thy God' (*Mic.* 6:8). Now the humiliation of wicked men is never joined with reformation. There is no walking with God. Josiah reformed himself and his people to outward obedience, as much as he could, but he had not their hearts at command.

3. Again, *Sin must appear bitter to the soul*, else we shall never be truly humbled for it. There is in every renewed soul a secret hatred and loathing of evil, which manifests the soundness both of true humiliation and reformation, and is expressed in three things.

(1.) In a serious purpose and resolution not to offend God in the least kind. The drunkard must purpose to leave his drunkenness, and the swearer resolve between God and his own heart, to forsake his base curses, and cry mightily herein for help from above.

(2.) Secondly, There must be a constant endeavour to avoid the occasions and allurements of sin. Thus

Job made a covenant with his eyes, that 'he should not look upon a maid' (*Job* 31:1); and thus every unclean and filthy person should make a covenant with themselves against the sins which they are most addicted unto. When they came to serve God, in Hosea, then 'away with idols' (*Hos.* 14:8). So must we, when we look heavenward, cast from us all our sins whatsoever.

(3.) Thirdly, There must be a hatred and loathing of sin in our confessions. We must confess it with all the circumstances, the time when, and place where. We must aggravate our offences, as David did: 'Against thee have I sinned, and done this evil in thy sight' (*Psa.* 51:4); and as the apostle: 'I was a blasphemer, I was a persecutor', I was thus and thus. He did not extenuate his sin, and say, the rulers commanded me so to do; but, 'I persecuted the church' out of the wickedness of mine own heart. A true Christian will not hide his sins, but lay them open, the more to abase himself before God. This aggravating of our sins will make them more vile unto us, and us more humble in the sight of them. True reformation of life is ever joined with an indignation of all sin, there is such a contrariety in the nature of a child of God against all evil.

[1.][4] We should therefore first *hate sin universally;* not one sin, but every kind of sin, and that most of all which most rules in us, and which is most prevalent in our own hearts. A sincere Christian hates sin in himself most. We must not hate that in another which we cherish in ourselves.

[2.] We should *hate sin the more, the nearer it comes to us,* in our children and friends, or any other way. It was David's fault to let Absalom his son go unreproved in his wicked practices, and Eli for not correcting his sons. We see what came of it, even their utter overthrow.

[3.] He that truly hates sin *will not think much to be admonished and reproved when he errs.* A man that hath a bad plant in his ground, that will eat out the heart of it, will not hate another that shall discover such an evil to him; so if anyone shall reprove thee for this or that sin, and thou hate him for it, it is a sign corruption is sweet to thee.

Only this caution must be remembered, reproof must not be given with a proud spirit, but in a loving, mild manner, with desire of doing good. There is a great deal of self-love in some men, who, instead of hating sin in themselves and others, approve and

---

[4] In margin of the original here, 'Signs of a true hatred of sin.'

countenance it, especially in great men, flattering them in their base humours, and fearing lest by telling them the truth they should be esteemed their enemies.

[4.] Our hatred of sin may be discerned *by our willingness to talk of it.*

He that hates a snake, or toad, will flee from it; so a man that truly abhors sin, will not endure to come near the occasions of it. What shall we say then of those that prostitute themselves to all sinful delights? As hatred of sin is in our affection, so it will appear in our actions. Those that love to see sin acted did never as yet truly loathe it.

It is a sign that we do not hate sin when we take not to heart the sins of our land. 'Woe is me that I am constrained to dwell in the tents of Kedar', saith David (*Psa.* 120:5); 'mine eyes gush out with tears because men keep not thy law' (*Psa.* 119:136). Lot's soul was vexed at the unclean conversation of the wicked (2 *Pet.* 2:7). But, alas! how do we come short of this! The greatest number are so far from mourning for the abominations of the land, that they rather set themselves against God in a most disobedient manner, and press others to sin against him. Are magistrates of David's mind, to labour to cut off all workers of iniquity from the land? Indeed, for small trifling things they will do a man justice, but where is the tenderness of God's glory? Where are those that seek to reform idolatry, Sabbath-breaking, and profaneness amongst us? Pity it is to see how many do hold the stirrup to the devil, by giving occasions and encouragements to others to commit evil. Do we hate sin, when we are like tinder, ready to receive the least motion to it, as our fashion-mongers, who transform themselves into every effeminate unbeseeming guise? Shall we say that these men hate sin, which, when they are reproved for it, labour to defend it or excuse it, counting their pride but comeliness, their miserable covetousness but thirst,[5] and drunkenness only good fellowship?

To strengthen our indignation against sin the better, consider,

1. *The ugliness thereof,* how opposite and distasteful it is to the Almighty, as appears in Sodom and in the old world. It is that for which God himself hates his own creature, and for which he will say to the wicked at the day of judgment, 'Go, ye cursed, into everlasting fire' (*Matt.* 25:41). Sin is the cause of all those diseases and crosses that befall the sons of men. It hath its rise from the devil, who is the father of it, and whose lusts we do whensoever we offend God.

---

[5] Perhaps should read 'thrift'?

There is not the least sin but it is committed against an infinite majesty, yea, against a good God, to whom we owe ourselves and all that we have, who waits when you will turn to him and live for ever; but if you despise his goodness, and continue still to provoke the eyes of his glory, is a terrible and revengeful[6] God, and ready every moment to destroy both body and soul in hell.

Sin is the bane of all comfort. That which we love more than our souls undoes us. It embitters every comfort, and makes that we cannot perform duties with spiritual life. Our very prayers are abominable to God so long as we live in known sin. What makes the hour of death and the day of judgment terrible but this?

2. Again, *Grow in the love of God*. The more we delight in him, the more we shall hate whatsoever is contrary to him. In that proportion that we affect God and his truth we will abhor every evil way, for these go together. Ye that love the Lord, hate the thing that is ill. The nearer we draw to him, the farther we are separated from everything below.

3. And to strengthen our indignation against sin, we should *drive our affections another way, and set them upon the right object*. A Christian should

---

[6] That is, 'avenging'.

consider, Wherefore did God give me this affection of love? Was it to set it on this or that lust, or any sinful course? Or hath he given me this affection of hatred that I should envy my brethren, and condemn the good way? No, surely I ought to improve every faculty of my soul to the glory of the giver, by loving that which he loves, and hating that which he hates. God's truth, his ways, and children, are objects worthy our love, and Satan with his deeds of darkness the fittest subjects of our indignation and hatred.

4. Fourthly, *True humiliation proceeds from faith,* and is in the faithful not only when judgment is upon them, but before the judgment comes, which they foreseeing by faith, do humble themselves. True humiliation quakes at the threatenings, for the very frowns of a father will terrify a dutiful child. As Josiah, when he did but hear of the threatenings against the land, he humbled himself in dust and ashes. 'He rent his clothes.' So true humiliation doth quake at the foresight of judgment, but the wicked never humble themselves but when the judgment is upon them. Carnal people are like men that, hearing thunder-claps afar off, are never a whit moved; but when it is present over their heads, then they tremble. So hypocrites care not for judgments afar off; as now when the church of God is in misery abroad we bless

ourselves, and think all is well. It is no thanks for a man to be humbled when the judgment is upon him, for so Pharaoh was, who yet, when the judgement was off, then he goes to his old bias again.

Let us try humiliation by these signs, whether we can willingly humble ourselves privately before God, and call ourselves to a reckoning; whether we add reformation of life to outward humiliation, when our heart doth tell us that we live in such and such sins; whether our hearts tremble at the threatenings, when we hear of judgments public or private. What is the ground that many deceive themselves? They say, if any judgment come upon them, then they will repent, and cry to God for mercy; and why should I deny myself of my pleasures of sin before? Oh, this is but a forced humiliation, not from love to God, but love to thyself. It is not free, therefore thou mayest go to hell with it. Others defer off their repentance till it be too late. When they have any sickness upon them they will cry to God for mercy. This is but Ahab's and Pharaoh's humiliation. It is not out of any love to God, but merely forced. It is too late to do it when God hath seized upon us by any judgment. Do it when he doth threaten, and now he hath seized upon the parts of the church abroad already; therefore now meet thy God by repentance.

5. A fifth difference between true humiliation and false is, that *with true humiliation is joined hope,* to raise up our souls with some comfort, else it is a desperation, not a humiliation. The devils do chafe, vex, and fret themselves, in regard of their desperate estate, because they have no hope. If there be no hope, it is impossible there should be true and sound humiliation; but true humiliation doth carry us to God, that what we have taken out of ourselves by humiliation, we may recover it in God. Therefore humility is such a grace, that though it make us nothing in ourselves, yet doth it carry us to God, who is all in all. Humiliation works between God and ourselves, and makes the heart leave itself, to plant and pitch itself upon God, and looks for comfort and assurance from him. And where there is not this there is no true humiliation. There is nothing more profitable in the world than humility, because, though it seem to have nothing, yet it carrieth the soul to him that fills all in all. Hence it is, that there is an abasing of ourselves for anything that we have done amiss, from love to God and love to his people, but yet it is joined with hope. We know God to be a gracious God unto us, and therefore we humble ourselves, and are grieved for offending of him.

6. A sixth difference between true humiliation and

false is this, *That hypocrites are sorrowful for the judgment that is upon them; but not for that which is the cause of the judgment,* which is sin; but the child of God, he is humbled for sin, which is the cause of all judgments. As good Josiah, when he heard read out of Deuteronomy the curses threatened for sin, and comparing the sins of his people with the sins against which the curses were threatened, he humbled himself for his sin and the sins of his people. For God's children know, if there were no iniquity in them, there should no adversity hurt them; and therefore they run to the cause, and are humbled for that. Whereas the wicked, they humble themselves only because of the smart and trouble which they do endure.

7. The last difference between true humiliation and false is this, *that true humiliation is a thorough humiliation.* Therefore it is twice repeated in this verse, '*thou didst humble thyself before God;* when thou heardest the words against this place, and against the inhabitants thereof, *and humbledst thyself before me.*' It is twice repeated in this verse, and afterward expressed by 'rending of clothes', and 'tears'. It was thorough humiliation. For he dwelt upon the humbling of his own soul. So that the children of God thoroughly humble themselves, but the hypocrite, when he doth humble himself, it is not

thoroughly. They count it a light matter. As soon as the judgment is off, they have forgotten their humiliation, as Pharaoh did. Many will heave a few sighs, and hang down the head like a bulrush for a time; but it is, like Ephraim's morning dew, quickly gone. They have no sound and thorough humiliation. It is but a mere offer of humiliation. Whereas the children of God, when they begin, they never cease working upon their own hearts with meditation, until they have brought their heart to a blessed temper, as we see in David, Ezra, Nehemiah, and Daniel, how they did humble themselves.

But why do God's children take pains in humbling themselves?

Partly because it must be done to purpose, else God will not accept it; and partly because there is a great deal of hardness and pride in the best, and much ado before a man can be brought for to humble himself. Therefore we must labour for this. We see what ado there was before Job could be brought to humble himself. Yet Job must be humbled before there comes 'one of a thousand' to comfort him (as *Job* 33:23). If a man be once thoroughly and truly humbled, he shall soon have comfort. By these marks we may know true humiliation from an humiliation counterfeit.

*Quest.* But here may arise another question, How may we know when we are humbled enough, or when we are grieved enough?

*Ans.* To this I answer, 1. That *there is not the same measure of humiliation required in all.* For those whom God did pick out for some great work, he doth more humble them than others, as he did Moses and Paul before he wrought the great work of converting the Gentiles. So David, before he came to be king, was a long time humbled.

2. Again, *There are others that have been greater sinners, and more openly wicked in their courses than others,* and in them a greater measure of humiliation is required.

3. Again, *There are others that are more tenderly brought up from childhood,* who have often renewed their repentance. These need not to be humbled so much as others; for humiliation should be proportionable unto the sinful estate of the soul; which because it differs in divers men, in like manner their humiliation ought to differ. But to answer the question more directly, we are said to be humbled enough,

1. First, *When we have wrought our souls to a hearty grief that we have offended God,* when we have a perfect and inward hatred of all sin, and when thou dost show the truth of thy grief by leaving off

thy sinful courses. So that, dost thou hate and leave thy sinful course? Then thou art sufficiently humbled. Go away with peace and comfort, thy sins are forgiven thee. Therefore it is not a slight humiliation that will serve the turn, but our hearts must be wrought unto a perfect hatred and leaving of all sins; for if this be not, we are not sufficiently humbled as yet. And when we find ourselves to hate and leave sin in some measure, then fasten our souls by faith, as much as may be, upon the mercy of God in Jesus Christ. For the soul hath two eyes, the one to look upon itself and our vileness, to humble us the more; the other, to fasten upon the mercy of God in Christ, to raise up our souls. For if the whole soul were fastened upon its own misery and vileness, then there could not be that humiliation which ought to be, neither could we serve God with such cheerfulness; therefore we must have our souls raised up to God's mercy. Now let us labour for the first, because the devil is so main an enemy unto it; for he knows well enough, that so much as we are humble and go out of ourselves to God, and rest upon him, so much we stand impregnable against his temptations, that he cannot prevail against us; and so much as we do not trust in God, but upon the creature, so much must we lie open to his snares. Therefore all his temptations tend to draw us to trust in the creature, to have a conceit of ourselves, and to draw our hearts from relying upon God. His first plot is always to make us rest in ourselves. Therefore let us labour to go out of ourselves, to see a vanity in ourselves, and a happiness in God, that so going out of ourselves, and relying upon God and his mercies, we may stand safe against Satan's temptations.

*Use.* This should teach us *to take heed of such affections as tend directly contrary to humiliation;* for how can it be but that those should be proud, that hold the doctrine of the Church of Rome, as, first, that we have no original sin in us, but it is taken away by baptism; that we are able to fulfil the law fully in this life. This is presumptuous. Whereas Paul cries out after baptism, 'O wretched man that I am, who shall deliver me from this body of death!' (*Rom.* 7:24). Nay, they can do more, namely, works of supererogation, whereby they merit heaven. How do these blow up the heart of man, and make it swell with pride! This must needs make men very proud, to think that a man can merit by works. With such blasphemous opinions they have infected the world, and led captive millions of souls into hell. Therefore let this be a rule of discerning true religion; for surely that is true religion which doth make us go out of ourselves; that takes away all from ourselves and gives all the glory to God; which makes us to plead for salvation by the mercy of God through the merits of Christ. But our religion doth teach us thus. Therefore it is the true religion, and will yield us sound comfort at the last. Thus much for inward humiliation, the humbling of ourselves, as Josiah did.

# 3

---

# THE ART OF MOURNING

*But because thine heart was tender, and thou didst
humble thyself before God, when thou heardest his
words against this place, and against the inhabitants
thereof, and humbledst thyself before me, and didst
rend thy clothes, and weep before me; I have even
heard thee also, saith the Lord.*

2 Chron. 34:27

A S the waters issuing from the sanctuary, mentioned by the prophet Ezekiel, grew deeper and
deeper; first to the ankles, then to the knees, and
after to the loins, until it came to an overflowing
river, so hath it fared with us in handling of this
text; wherein, from tenderness of heart, we have
waded deeper and deeper through the mysteries of

humiliation in the inward man, until at length from thence we are broken forth to the outward expressions of Josiah's inward humiliation, his 'rending of his clothes', and overflowing floods of 'tears'; which sprung partly from his apprehension of ruin at hand, to come upon God's sanctuary, and partly from the sorrow and sense of sin in himself and the people, as causes of his fear.

But to come to the text now read in your hearing, 'And didst rend thy clothes and weep before me', here we have set down the outward expression of Josiah's inward humiliation.

For true humiliation shows itself as well outwardly as inwardly. Now, the outward expression of his inward affection is set down in two things:

1. By rending of his clothes; 2. By his weeping.

No doubt but he did express his sorrow as well by words as by these gestures, although they be not here set down with the other; for he might for the time be surprised with so great a measure of sorrow and grief, as could not be expressed presently at that instant, or we may conceive that for the time he was so thoroughly humbled, that he could not speak orderly. Wherefore God did regard and look more to his affections and tears than to his words, for he rent his clothes and wept before God. As it is written of the poor publican, that he could not say much, and looked down with his eyes, saying, 'Lord, be merciful to me a sinner' (*Luke* 18:13); and as it was with the poor woman in the gospel who came to Christ weeping, and washed his feet with her tears, yet she said nothing (*Luke* 7:38); and as when Christ, upon the cock's third crowing, looked upon Peter, we find not what he said, but that he went out and wept bitterly (*Luke* 22:61–62); so here, we may imagine Josiah's affection was too full of sorrow to speak distinctly and composedly; for from a troubled soul can proceed nothing but troubled words; from a broken heart comes broken language. But howsoever, likely it is that Josiah did speak somewhat; for God saith, 'I have even also heard thee.' But to leave this and come to the outward expressions here set down, let us learn somewhat from his rending of his clothes and weeping.

'Rending of clothes' was a thing frequently used in old times, as we see in the Scriptures; and it was a visible representation of the inward sorrow of the heart. Job rent his clothes (*Job* 1:20); his friends rent their clothes (*Job* 2:12); Paul and Barnabas rent theirs (*Acts* 14:14); the high priest rent his clothes, being to accuse Christ (*Mark* 14:63); and Hezekiah rent his clothes when he heard the words of Rabshakeh

(*Isa.* 37:1). Nay, this was a common action, and frequently used among the heathen also; for they likewise, upon any disastrous accident, were used to rend their clothes; as we read of a heathen king, that having his city invaded round about with enemies, rent his clothes.[1] So that it hath been the custom both of God's church and also of heathen, to rend their clothes. But what is the ground or reason of this? The reason of such their rending of clothes was, because that in their sorrow they thought themselves unworthy to wear any. They forgat all the comforts of this life; as holy Josiah forgets his estate, his throne, his royal majesty, and crown. He looks up to the great God, and considers duly whom he stood under, and the miserable estate of the people, over whom he was governor; and thereupon he rends his clothes, showing hereby that he was unworthy of those ornaments wherewith he was covered. We know that clothes have divers uses; as,

1. First, For *necessity,* to cover our nakedness, and to preserve from the injuries of the weather.

2. Secondly, Clothes are given for *distinction of sexes and degrees:* to know the great man from the mean, the woman from the man.

---

[1] Perhaps a reference to the Sultan—'the raging Turk' of the Puritans—in his anguish at the siege of Scodra. Cf. among others Trapp on Ezra 9:3.

3. And lastly, *They serve for ornaments* to honour our vile flesh, which is so base that it must fetch ornaments from base creatures. Now, so far as they served for ornaments, he rent his clothes, as thinking himself unworthy of any garments; for he being in grief doth rend his clothes, thinking with himself, why should I stand upon clothes and outward things to cover me? God is angry. Till he be appeased I will take no pleasure in any earthly thing. Therefore, apprehending the wrath of God, he rent his clothes. Well, this is but an outward expression, and therefore it must proceed from inward truth. This rending of clothes was a national ceremony, which seeing we have not used amongst us, we must rend our hearts with grief. For the rending of clothes shows the rending of the heart before, without which there is no acceptance with God; for the rending of the clothes without the rending of the heart is but hypocrisy; as *Joel* 2:13, he says, 'Rend your hearts, and not your garments, ye hypocrites.' So that outward expressions of sorrow are no further good, than when they come from inward grief and affection. Now, when both these are joined together it is a comely thing; for wherein stands comeliness but when all the parts of our body do agree in proportion, when one limb is not bigger than another? So it is uncomely and

an hypocritical thing for a man to have all outward expression and yet to have no inward grief. This is but acting of humiliation, when we hang down the head like a bulrush, and the heart is not sound. But outward expressions are good when the heart is grieved to purpose; when they proceed from inward humiliation.

*Quest.* And why ought this to be?

*Ans.* Because both body and soul have a part in the action of sin. Therefore it is needful that they should be joined in humiliation for sin. There is no sin of the body but the soul hath part in it, nor any sin in the soul but the body hath part in it. Therefore both body and soul should be humbled together. Labour then to have outward expressions and shows of sorrow come from a true sorrowful heart. There be two things in the religious actions of men.

1. There is the outward action or expression.

2. There is the inward, which gives life to the other.

The outward is easy, and subject to hypocrisy. It is an easy matter to rend clothes and to force tears, but it is a hard matter to afflict the soul. The heart of man taketh the easiest ways, and lets the hardest alone, thinking to please God with that. But God will not be served so; for he must have the inward affections, or else he doth abhor the outward actions. Therefore let us as well labour for humble hearts as humble gestures. We must rend our hearts and not our clothes, when we come into the presence of God. We must labour, as to show humility, so to have humility, that so we be not like hypocrites, who make show of a great deal of devotion in carriage, but yet have none in heart; a great deal of outward humiliation, whenas they have none within.

The papists are wicked and erroneous in all their devotions, especially in the point of justification, and in other points of the worship of God; for is it not a superstitious error, to think to please God with outward observations, when they do not come from inward truth? Their religion is all an outside, consisting merely of outward performances. But true devotion, the Scripture teacheth, cometh from a heart judicially understanding the case of its own self; considering what a great God it hath to deal withal, a God full of glory and majesty. Doth God love blind sacrifices? No. Devotion must come from the heart, and spread itself from thence into the countenance and carriage. For then it is true, when the outward expression doth show the inward disposition.

*Use.* This reproves the negligence of people in these times. Where is their inward humiliation? Nay, where is their outward humiliation? In popery, there is an acting of humiliation. They whip themselves in their bodies, and other such outward fooleries and gestures they have in their hypocritical devotions. Thus do they in some sort humble themselves. But how few there are amongst us that humble themselves in apprehension of their own misery, who yet, if they look to their own persons, have cause enough! Yea, and how few are there that are humbled for the miseries of the church abroad! Where shall we find a mourning soul?

Well, seeing it is not a custom amongst us to rend our clothes, yet let us make conscience of being proud in apparel; for it is a wicked and a fearful thing when men will regard some wicked and foolish fashion, and set more by it than by God's favour, threatenings, and judgments abroad. Many there are that, instead of rending their clothes, come into God's house to show their bravery;[2] to see and to be seen. Where they should most of all humble themselves, there they come to show their pride, even before God. Whereas they should come to hear the voice of the great God of heaven, and stand in his presence, who is a 'consuming fire'. Before whom the very angels cover their faces and the earth trembles, they, contrariwise, come

---

[2] That is, in the sense of 'finery', 'showy dress'.

to outface and provoke him with their pride. We see Josiah, though he were a king, he rent his clothes, forgot all his bravery, and considers himself not so much a king over the people, over whom God had set him, as a subject to God. Wherefore, though, as I said, the custom of rending of clothes be not used in our church, yet let us ever make conscience of rending our hearts, and so to make our peace with God, as this good king did. It follows:

'And weptest before me.'

In which words is set down *the second outward expression of Josiah's inward humiliation,* which is 'weeping'. This came nearer to him than rending of clothes, for it touched his body. Hence, in a word, observe,

*Doct.* 1. *That the body and soul must join together in the action of humiliation,* for the soul and body go together in the acting of sin, therefore they must go together in humiliation. As they were both made by God, and redeemed by Christ, so they sin and practise good together. Now I will show three ways wherein the soul and body have communion one with another, whereby it may appear how reasonable and fitting a thing it is they should be both humbled together.

1. First, The soul and body have communion together *by way of impression or information;* for

sensible things have an impression upon the senses, and so come into the soul; for nothing comes into it but through the senses of the body; because, though the soul may imagine golden mountains, and things that it never saw, yet the working of the soul depends upon the body, for the body informs it of all outward objects. As the body is beholding to the soul for the ruling and guiding of it, so the soul is beholding to the body for many things; as now in the very sacrament, God helps the soul with the senses; Christ, as it were, in the sacrament enters through the senses more lively than in the preaching of the word, for there he enters in by the ears, but in the sacrament he is seen, tasted, handled, felt. So that the soul and body have communion together by way of information.

2. Secondly, The soul and body have communion together *by way of temptation,* for the soul standing in need of many outward things which are pleasing and delightful, and having sympathy with the body, it is led away by the body. Outward objects are pleasing to the senses of carnal men. Now these passing through the senses into the soul, it is led away, and so they become a dangerous temptation.

3. Thirdly, The soul and the body have communion together, both in sinful and in good actions, *by way of subjection or execution;* for God hath made

the body, with the parts thereof, to be the instruments and weapons of the soul. The body is a house wherein the soul is kept. It is a shop for the soul. Now the soul useth the body, with the members thereof, as instruments or weapons, either to honour God or dishonour him. The wicked fight against God with all the members of their body, with their eyes, tongue, feet, hands. Now the body having thus a part in sin, as well as the soul, therefore it is necessary that the body and soul should join together in humiliation.

*Caution.* Here we must take heed of a notable sleight of the devil in popery. The papists think the body only in fault for sin, and therefore they humble and afflict their bodies for it, while they puff up their soul with pride, a conceit of merit and satisfaction. They are falsely humble and truly proud, while they afflict the body and omit the soul. They are falsely humbled, because they humble their body only; but truly proud, because they think by afflicting and humbling their bodies to merit. But let us take heed of this gross error, and remember to let both soul and body join in the work.

*Doct.* 2. The second thing here to be noted is, that *when God will afflict or humble a man, it is not a kingdom that will save him.* As Josiah, though he were a monarch, — for he was an absolute monarch, — yet if God threaten, his kingdom can do him no good. If God will abase men, whether they be his children or enemies, it is not a kingdom can protect them. When God showed Belshazzar the handwriting upon the wall, he could take no comfort in anything (*Dan.* 5:5–6); yea, his dear children, if he show but tokens of his displeasure against them, though they be kings, as Josiah was, yet he can humble them. If God roar, it is not their greatness can keep them; if not now, yet he will make them to tremble hereafter.

*Doct.* 3. The third thing here that we learn from the example of Josiah, being a king, is, *That tears and mourning for sin, when it comes from inward grief, is a temper well befitting any man.* It is a carriage befitting a king. It is not unbeseeming any, of what sex or degree soever. It is no womanish or base thing. When one hath to deal with God, he must forget his estate and take the best way to meet with God. This is evident by many instances, for David, though a man of war, yet when he had to deal with God he watered his couch with his tears (*Psa.* 6:6). So Hezekiah, though a great king, yet he humbled himself (*Isa.* 38:1ff.). Nay, our blessed Saviour himself did it 'with strong cries and tears' (*Heb.* 5:7), when he had to deal with God.

*Use.* This serves *for the justification of this holy abasement and humbling of ourselves.* When we have to deal with God, then all abasement is little enough. 'I will be yet more vile than thus', saith holy David (2 *Sam.* 6:22). So let us say when we have to deal with God; I will be yet more vile, and so cast ourselves down before the Lord. All expression of devotion is little enough, so it be without hypocrisy. Yet I pray give me leave once again to give warning unto you concerning outward actions, for most have conceived wrong of devotion and humiliation. They think that devotion is only in outward actions; as in outward act to hear a little, to read, confer, or pray a little, whereas in truth these outward acts do only make up the body of devotion, which, without the soul, namely, the inward religious affection, looking unto God, is no better than a dead carrion. Our outward expression must come from the apprehension of the goodness, mercy, and justice of God, before whom the very angels veil their faces. It is not outward devotion that will serve the turn, as to come to the church with this bare conceit and forethought; I will go pray, and kneel, and express all outward carriage, in the meantime neglecting to stir up the soul to worship God with these or like thoughts; I will go to the place where God is, where his truth is, where his angels are, to hear that word whereby I shall be judged at the last day. Therefore let all holy actions come from within first, and thence to the outward man. Let us work upon our hearts a consideration of the goodness, justice, majesty, and mercy of God, and then let there be an expression in body, such as may bring men off from their sins; for else there is a spirit of superstition that will draw men far from God in seeming services, conceiving that God will accept of outward and formal expressions only.

Well, we see that weeping and mourning for sins is a carriage not unbeseeming for a king. Therefore it is a desperate madness not to humble ourselves and be abased, now we have to deal with God. Your desperate atheists of the world will not tremble at threatenings, nor humble themselves till death comes, which humbles them and makes them tremble; whereas, on the contrary, that soul which, feeling the wrath of God, humbles itself betimes, and trembles at threatenings, that soul, I say, — when the great judgment of death comes, and appearance before God, — looks death in the face with comfort; whereas your desperate atheists, that can now scorn God, swear at every word, and blaspheme God to his face; let God but show his displeasure, they tremble and quake upon any noise of fear. Therefore when we have to deal with God, it is wisdom, and the ground of all courage, to humble and abase ourselves with fear, as Josiah did although he were a king.

'And thou didst weep before me.'

His tender heart did melt itself into tears. In the first clause of the verse you have his tender heart set down, and here we have *the melting of the tender heart*. There we have the cloud, here we have the shower. Therefore I will speak something of the original of tears. We know that tears are strained from the inward parts, through the eyes; for the understanding first conceiveth cause of grief upon the heart, after which the heart sends up matter of grief to the brain, and the brain being of a cold nature, doth distil it down into tears; so that if the grief be sharp and piercing, there will follow tears after from most. But to come to the particulars; we see the provoking cause of tears, from without, in Josiah, was the danger of his kingdom, hearing the judgment of God threatened against his country and place. Whence, for the instruction of magistrates, I will enforce this point.

*Doct.* 4. *That it concerns magistrates above all others, to take to heart any danger whatsoever, that is upon their people;* for as kings are set above all other people in place, so they should be above them in goodness and grace. They ought, above all others, to take to heart any judgment, either upon them already, or feared; as good Josiah did, whom, while he looked not so much to himself and his own good, as to that state whereof he was king, the very threatenings of judgment against it, made to express his grief with tears. The bond that knits the king to the people, and the people to the king, requires this; for kings are heads, and shepherds over the people. Now the shepherd watcheth over his flock; the head is quickly sensible of any hurt of the body; all the senses are provident for the body. So it should be with all great persons in authority. They should cherish the good estate of the subjects as their own; for they are committed to their care. And even as the head doth care for the body, and forecast for it, so those that are in authority should forecast for any good to the body of the commonwealth. An excellent example of this we have in holy David; who, when there was a judgment coming upon his people, 'Lord,' saith he, 'let the judgment come upon me and my father's house; what have these sheep done?' (2 *Sam.* 24:17). And surely such magistrates as are tenderly affected with the case of those under them, shall lose nothing by it; for the people likewise will carry a tender affection towards them again. As we see, when the people went to fight against Absalom, they would not let David go with them, but they said to him, 'Thou art worth ten thousand of us' (2 *Sam.* 18:3); that is, they had rather that ten thousand of them should die in the battle, than that David should have any hurt come to him; so he lost nothing for his love and affection towards the people, for they showed the like love to him in his distress. So likewise when Josiah was dead, the people wept largely for him (for with him perished all the glory of that flourishing kingdom), as we may read in the story (2 *Chron.* 35:24–25, compared with *Zech.* 12:11). They mourned for him with an exceeding great mourning, in Hadadrimmon, in the valley of Megiddo. So that there is no love lost between the magistrate and the people; for if the magistrate be tenderly affected to them, the people will likewise weep for him again, and lament his case in his distress. But now to come to a more general instruction, we will leave speaking of Josiah as king, and take him into consideration as an holy man, and make him a pattern unto us all, of whatsoever civil condition we be; and so we learn this point,

*Doct.* 5. *That it is the duty of every Christian to take to heart the threatenings of God against the place and people where he doth live;* to take to heart the afflictions and miseries of the church and commonwealth, the grievances of others as well as his own. The mourning and weeping of Josiah was for the estate of the church, when he heard the judgment threatened against the place and inhabitants thereof. There be tears of compassion for ourselves and for others. There were both of them in Josiah; for no doubt but he wept for himself and his own sins, and over and above his own had special tears of compassion for his people. Thus then it becomes a Christian that will have the reward of Josiah, to abase his heart as he did for the estate of the church.

Good Nehemiah took to heart the grief of his country. The joy of his own preferment did not so much glad him, as the grief for his nation the Jews cast him down. What joy can a true heart have, now the church of God is in affliction? We are all of one house. When one part of the house is a-fire, the other part had need to look to itself. There were many things wrought upon the heart of Josiah, which caused him to weep; so there are many causes should move us, as the seeing of the sins that are committed in the land ought to make us grieve, and to express our grief one way or other.

And the love of Christ, were it in us, would make us mourn; as when we hear God blasphemed, and his name dishonoured, and when we see the people bent to idolatry; how can this but break even a heart of stone? Nay, a gracious heart will mourn and weep for the judgment of God upon wicked men, considering them as men, and as the creatures of God. Thus Christ wept for the wicked Jews in Jerusalem, though they were his enemies: 'O Jerusalem, Jerusalem, *etc.*' (*Luke* 19:41, *Matt.* 23:37); and so good Jeremiah, though he were ill used, and exceedingly abused by the people, yet he saith, 'Oh that my head were water, and mine eyes a fountain of tears, that I might weep day and night for them' (*Jer.* 9:1). Though they had wronged, persecuted, and counted him a contentious fellow, only because he taught the truth of God; yet such was the affection of tender-hearted Jeremiah, that he desired that he might weep day and night for them. But continual weeping must have a lasting spring affording continual issues of tears, which Jeremiah not finding in himself (such is the dryness of every man's heart, that it is soon emptied of tears), and thereupon fearing he should not weep enough, he doth earnestly desire it, and if hearty wishes may obtain, he would have it to be supplied with a plentiful measure of tears in his lamentation for the ensuing calamity of his people: 'O that mine head were a well of water, and mine eyes a fountain of tears, that I might weep day and night for the slain of the daughter of my people!'

*Quest*. But why did not Jeremiah rather pray that they had a fountain of tears to weep for themselves?

*Ans*. Because he, knowing the hardness of their hearts, thought it to no end to entreat them to weep for themselves. Their hearts were harder than the nether millstone. They never desired it, yet he weeps for them. Thus we see how godly men have been formerly affected, and [that] it is our duty even to weep and mourn for the very wicked. We have matter enough of lamentation and weepings at this day, if we look abroad; and at home, if we look to judgments felt and feared, we have cause to weep, before the decree come out against us. Therefore we should meet God beforehand. It is no thank for a man to be humbled when the judgment is come upon him; but when we can weep before the judgment is come, it is a sign of faith. Happy were we if faith could make us do that which sense makes wicked men to do. If the believing of the judgment before it come would make us seek unto God, oh how God would love such a one! This should teach us every one to mourn; and indeed a Christian soul cannot but do it, and that for divers reasons.

1. First, *Because of that sympathy between the Head and the members*. A Christian hath the spirit of

Christ, who takes to heart the miseries of the church. Now, can that spirit of Christ be in any, and he not affected as Christ in heaven is affected? Surely no.

2. Again, It must needs be so in regard of *the communion which is between the members of the body*. We are all a part of one mystical body, whereof Christ is the head. What member can he be of this body that doth not take to heart the miseries of the other members? There is want of life where there is no sense of misery.

3. Thirdly, Where there is true grace there will be weeping and mourning for the church, in regard of *the insolency of the church's enemies* and their blasphemous speeches. Where is now their God? their religion? What is now become of their Reformation? What child can hear the reproach and dishonour of God his Father without bowels of compassion?

4. Again, A gracious man will weep in regard of *the danger of not mourning;* for by not mourning we have a kind of guilt lying upon us, for we make the sins and miseries of the church our own, as Paul tells the Corinthians, reproving them for not mourning (*1 Cor.* 5:2). Therefore as we are a part of the body, so we must have a part of the shame and grief. Again, God hath promised to mark and single out all those that mourn for the sins of the time; therefore, on the

contrary, those that do not mourn are in a dangerous estate (*Ezek.* 9:4).

5. Again, We must add *reformation unto lamentation,* else the whole church and commonwealth is in danger. If Achan be not sought out and punished, the whole state is in danger, and lies open to the wrath of God.

For these reasons we ought to take to heart the sins and miseries of the times; for the Spirit of God is in every Christian, that will not suffer him otherwise to be, than to weep and mourn for his own sins, and for the sins and miseries of others.

*Use* 1. If this be so, what will become of those that take not to heart nor mourn for the miseries of the church? that judge not aright of the poor, but censure the judgment of the afflicted, add affliction to the afflicted and misery to the miserable? What shall we say to those that are so far from helping God, that they help the enemies of God, and are grieved at the heart to hear any cause of comfort on the church's part? whose hearts it doth joy to hear of any overthrow on the church's side? Such false hearts there are, and many that are glad of the sins of others, thinking thereby to hide their own wicked courses. These men are far from mourning. Let our souls also be far from entering into their secrets.

*Use* 2. If this be so, that holy men ought to take to heart and weep for the judgments of the commonwealth, both felt and feared, and also for the judgment of God upon the churches abroad, then

*Quest.* How may we get this weeping and mourning for others? I answer,

*Ans.* 1. First, *Remove the impediments that hinder;* as, first, a hard and stony heart, which is opposite to tenderness. Josiah had a melting heart, and therefore it was soon dissolved into tears. Our hearts are worse than brass or stone, for workmen can work upon them; but nothing will work upon the hard heart of man. All the judgments in the world will not work upon it; for all the Israelites saw the judgments of God in Egypt, and all his mercies and blessings unto them in the wilderness, yet it would not work upon them, because they had hard hearts. Therefore let us get a good spring of tears, that is, a soft and tender heart, and let us beg it of God, for it is his promise to give us tender hearts; and then there will be an easy expression of it in the outward man.

2. The second, *Let us beware of the love of earthly things, and get a heart truly loving towards God;* for love is compared to fire; and fire, among many other properties it hath, melts the gold, and makes it pliable. Heat is the organ of the soul, whereby it doth

anything, and the instrument of nature. So spiritual heat, a warm soul, warmed with the love of God and of our Christian brethren, will make the heart pliable, and melt into tears. Therefore get a loving heart, filled with love to God and Christian brethren, that we may mortify self-love, which dries up the soul. There can be no melting in such a self-loved soul. Let us therefore labour for spiritual love, to cross and subdue carnal self-love. It is this blessed heat that must send forth this heavenly water of tears; it is the spirit of love that must yield this distillation from the broken heart; this works all heavenly affection in us. Therefore Christ compriseth all the commandments under love. And indeed that is all.

3. Thirdly, If we would have our souls fit to grieve, *let us be content to see as much as we can, with our own eyes, the miseries of others.* The best way to weep is to enter into the house of mourning, and set before our eyes the afflictions of others. The very sight of misery is a means to make the soul weep. And let us be willing to hear that which we cannot see; as Nehemiah was content to hear, nay, to inquire, concerning the church abroad; and when he heard that it was not well with them it made him weep. Every man will cry, What news? But where is the man, when he hears of the news beyond the seas,

that sends up sighs to God in prayer, that he would take pity upon his church? It is a good way to use our senses, to help our souls to grieve.

4. Again, *Let us read [of] the estate of God's church*, what it hath been from the beginning of the world; what miseries God's children have endured in former ages by reason of war and the like, that so we may work grief upon own hearts. We have always matter of grief while we are in this world; if we look abroad, we shall find matter of mourning. And surely we should labour to mourn if we desire to be blessed. For 'blessed are they that mourn: they shall be comforted' (*Matt.* 5:4).

5. Fifthly, That we may get this weeping and mourning, *let us work this tender affection upon our own hearts*. The soul hath a faculty to work upon itself. Therefore let us shame ourselves for our own deadness, dryness, and spiritual barrenness this way, that we can yield no sighs, no tears for God, for his church and glory. Let us reason thus with our souls: If I should lose my wife, or child, or my estate, this naughty heart of mine would weep and be grieved; but now there is greater cause of mourning for myself and the church of God, and yet I cannot grieve. Augustine saith he could weep for her that killed herself out of love to him, but he could not weep for

his own want of love to God.[3] We have many that will weep for the loss of friends, wealth, and such like things, but let them lose God's favour, be in such an estate there is but one step between them and hell, they are never grieved nor moved at it. Therefore, seeing they do not weep for themselves, let us weep for them. Can we weep when we see a man hurt in his body, and ought we not much more for the danger of his soul? Therefore let us work this sorrow upon our hearts. Now, we are to receive the sacrament, which is a feast, and therefore must be eaten cheerfully. The passover was a banquet, and therefore to be eaten with joy, but withal it was used to be eaten with sour herbs. So must it be in this blessed banquet which God hath provided for our souls. There must be sorrow as well as joy. It is a mixed action, and therefore it must be eaten with sour herbs, presenting to the eyes of our mind the object of the old Adam; thinking upon the vileness of our nature, that have such filthy speeches, disobedient actions, such rebellious thoughts in us. Great need have I of the mercy and favour of God to look upon such a defiled soul as I am. And also, having in the eyes of our soul Christ crucified, look upon Christ, which is crucified in the sacrament, sacramentally. What was

[3] Augustine on the death of his mother Monica.

that which broke the body of Christ? Was it not sin? That sin which I so often cherish, this pride, this envy, unbelief, and hypocrisy, this covetousness of mind was that which put Christ into such torment. It was not the nails, but my sins. The sacrament must work upon our hearts so as to work grief in us. We must weep as the people did for Josiah, according as God hath promised we should do. It is said, 'They shall look on him whom they have pierced by their sins, and weep and mourn for him as one that mourneth for his only son' (*Zech.* 12:10). So then, the sacrament is not only a matter of joy and thanks, but a matter of sorrow. Therefore, if we would joy in the sacrament, let us first be humbled for sin, and then joy in it afterwards.

*Obj.* But here it might be objected, Are we not bid for to rejoice always? and always to be thankful? (*1 Thess.* 5:16, 18). Then how can these agree? for weeping and mourning are contrary to thanksgiving and joy.

*Ans.* To this I answer, that the estate of a Christian in this life is a mixed estate, both inward and outward; his outward estate and the inward disposition of the soul is mixed. Therefore, having this mixed estate, our carriage must [be] answerable; as we have always cause of mourning and rejoicing both from that in us and from without us, therefore a Christian ought to rejoice always, and in some measure to mourn always. As, for example,

A Christian hath cause of mourning within him when he looks upon his sinful nature and the sins which he doth daily commit, yet notwithstanding, at the same time, there is cause of joy, and great reason to bless God, when he considers that God hath pardoned his sins in Christ. Thus the apostle did (*Rom.* 7:24); when he looked upon himself and his own vileness, he cries out, 'O wretched man that I am, who shall deliver me from this body of death?'; yet for all this, at the same time he rejoiceth and blesseth God: 'I thank God through Jesus Christ my Lord, who hath freed me from the law of sin and of death.' Thus, you see, we have always in respect of ourselves both cause of joy and mourning, therefore we must do both. So have we in like manner continual causes both of joy and sorrow from without us, if we look to the church of God: of joy, in regard there is a God in heaven who hath an eye to his church, who pitieth it and tendereth[4] it as the apple of his eye; that takes to heart the afflictions of it; that will be glorious in the midst of the troubles of his people, by upholding, comforting, and turning all to the best for them;—of

---

[4] That is, 'guardeth it'.

sorrow also, in respect of the miseries under which the church of God doth groan, of which we are bound to take notice, and so to weep with them that weep (*Isa.* 22:12; *Amos* 6:6; *Rom.* 12:15). You see the rare mixture of joy and sorrow in a Christian, whereby he is made capable of this great privilege, as neither to be swallowed up of grief, because that his sorrow proceeds from a heart where there is cause of joy, nor to lose himself in excessive joy, because he always sees in himself cause of sorrow. Now, as it is to be seen in other mixtures that there is not at all times an equal quantity or portion of each particular thing to be mingled, but now more of the one, and at another time more of the other, according as the cause doth vary, so is it in this mixture of joy and sorrow for ourselves and for others; sometimes joy must abound with the causes of it, and sometimes sorrow with its causes doth superabound. It will be worth our inquiry, therefore, to know when to joy most, and when to weep most, which we shall know by God's call in outward occasions, and by the spirit of discretion within us, which will guide us. For God hath given his children a spirit of discretion, that will teach them when to joy and when to weep most. As God calls to mourning now in these times that the church of God is in misery, as he calls for sighs for the afflictions of Joseph, so the spirit of discretion within us doth tell us what to do.

*Quest.* Yet here may be a question, How shall we know when to cease and leave off mourning? for the soul is a finite thing, and cannot dwell upon one action always, because it hath many things to do; and therefore it cannot always mourn nor always rejoice.

*Ans.* To this I answer, that we have mourned enough, and discharged our duty sufficiently therein, when we have overcome our hearts, and brought them to a temper of mourning, and have complained before God, spread the ill of the times before him, and entreated pity from him, having poured out ourselves in prayer, though short, yet effectual. When we have this done, then we have discharged our duty in mourning, and may turn to other occasions as God doth require of us; for when we have mourned and wept, then we must look upon causes of rejoicing and thanksgiving. We must always remember so to mourn and weep that yet notwithstanding, looking upon God's blessing upon us both in kingdom, state, and our own particular persons, we may be excited to thankfulness; for we must not always be sullen, looking upon the evil, but casting our eyes upon the good things we do enjoy, we must provoke ourselves to be thankful. Even as men that have their eyes dazzled will look upon some green colour to recover their sight again, so when we have wrought upon our souls and brought them to mourn, then to help and raise them up, we ought to look upon causes of joy and thankfulness. We have cause of thankfulness when we consider that many churches in France and other places are invaded by enemies, oppressed with cruelty, and deprived of liberty, while yet we enjoy the liberty and free passage of the gospel, being freed from the destruction of war and pestilence, which devoureth so many that it makes the land to mourn. He continueth to us liberty to hear the word, and gives us many blessings which others have not. Nay, we have cause to bless God for freeing us from that terriblest judgment of all judgments—which makes both church and commonwealth to mourn—because he doth not suffer us to fall into the hands of man, but takes us into his own hand to correct. It is God's infinite mercy that he doth not humble us by our enemies, but takes us into his own hand. Therefore let us not provoke him, lest he give us up to the hands of our merciless enemies, which is a terrible judgment. We had better an hundred times meet him by repentance, and cast ourselves into his hands, for then we have only to deal with a merciful God; but when we are to deal with merciless men that scorn the gospel, then we have both God and them to deal with, which doubles our affection.[5]

Therefore let us mourn, seeing we have cause, for ourselves and the estates of others; but yet let us be thankful, for if we would be more thankful for God's benefits, we should have them longer continued. For, as prayer begs blessings, so thanksgiving continues them. As the best way to obtain good things is prayer and mourning, so the best way to preserve them is thanksgiving and rejoicing. So, then, we have plainly seen that Christians should not always be dumpish and look sourly, but they must as well rejoice and be thankful, as mourn and weep.

*Quest.* 1. But here, ere I proceed, I must answer some cases of conscience. As, first, What shall we say to those souls that cannot weep for the sins and miseries of the church, and therefore complain for the want of it?

Secondly, What shall we say to that soul that can weep, but more for outward than for spiritual things?

*Sol.* 1. To the first I answer briefly, that we must not speak friar-like of tears, and never know from whence they come. But when we speak of weeping,

[5] 'affliction'?

we must always understand that tears are no further good than when they spring from sorrow and love within, than when they proceed from inward hatred to sin, and from fear and love to the church of God. If this be in a man, the matter is not much for tears. There may be weeping without true sorrow, as there was in Esau for the blessing (*Gen.* 27:38); and so the Jews, they could weep and howl upon their beds when there was a famine, yet there was no sound sorrow in them.

And, on the contrary, there may be true sorrow without weeping, yea, and such may it be that there can be no weeping, because their sorrow may be so great that it is rather an astonishment than a weeping. In a fresh wound in the body, at the first there is not such pain felt nor the blood seen, because the part is astonied only; so the soul for a time may be in such an astonishment and grief that there may be no expression of tears. Again, the soul doth follow the temperature of the body. Some are of a more easy constitution to shed tears than others, so that there may be more grief where there are fewest tears.

But to come to the question more directly, we ought to think our estates not so good as they should be, if we cannot at one time or other weep for the sins and miseries of the church. If we can shed tears for outward things at one time or other, and cannot weep for spiritual, it is a bad sign; for certainly, one time or other ordinarily God's children express their sorrow for their sins, and the estate of the church, by tears. They either have tears for spiritual respects, or else they mourn that they cannot mourn, grieve that they cannot grieve, and desire that they might mourn and that they could weep. They wish with Jeremiah that their head were a fountain of tears, they wish they might have their bodies to answer the intent of their soul, that so they might largely express outwardly their inward grief. As Jeremiah feared he should not have tears enough, therefore wished that his head were a fountain of tears, so they desire, Oh that I could mourn, and that I could weep!

*Sol.* 2. But what shall we say to those that can weep for other things? Shall they be condemned for hypocrites?

1. I answer, No; for a torrent may run faster for the present than a continual current; so on the sudden there may be tears and grief for outward things, but yet grief for sin is more because of the continuance thereof. For sin is a continual cause of sorrow. Whereas sorrow for outward things is but on a sudden, as it was in David when he cried, 'Oh my son Absalom, my son Absalom!' (2 *Sam.* 18:33). What ado is here on the

sudden for Absalom! but yet he wept for his sins more, because that was a continual grief. So in a Christian, there may be some sudden passion, when he may seem to weep and grieve most for outward things, but yet his grief for sin and the misery of the church is more, because it is a continual grief.

2. Again, Spiritual grief comes from spiritual causes. Tears for sin, and for the church of God, do issue merely from spiritual grounds; whereas in natural grief for outward things, we have both the Spirit and nature that make us grieve. Now when both these meet together, they carry the soul strongly, as in a stream. So that there must needs be more tears and grief for outward things. As when the windows of heaven were opened from above, and the foundations below were broken up, there must needs follow a great flood (*Gen.* 7:11); so when we have the Spirit from above, and our nature below, there must of necessity be a great grief for outward things. But yet in these cases, a little of spiritual sorrow is better than a great deal of natural, for spiritual grief fats the soul. As the river Nile runs through Egypt, and fats the land, so this heavenly water of tears and grief fattens the soul, and makes it fit for all holy services. They are both good, but one less than the other. Natural grief is allowable, which if a man have not, he is in

a reprobate sense; for the apostle reckons this up as a great sin, that in the latter days men should be without natural affection. So then we see, that for this reason also there may be a great store of grief and tears for outward things.

3. Again, Let them that grieve that they cannot more grieve, know and comfort themselves, that they have the Spirit of God within them, which is an everlasting spring that will in time overcome all carnal and worldly respects whatsoever, and make the heart in a fit temper of weeping and grieving for spiritual respects.

*Use.* Well, if this be thus, what shall we think of the jovial people of the world, who are so far from this sorrow, that—when a man shall come and ask them when they wept for their sins, when they did ever mourn and send up sighs to God for their swearing, lying, profanation of God's Sabbath, for the wrong they have done to others, or for any of their sins—the time was never yet wherein they ever shed a tear for sin, or had a sigh, groan, or mourning for sin? What estate are we born in? All children of wrath, and heirs of damnation. But when got you out of this state? You have ever lived in jollity. Therefore as yet you are as you were born, a child of wrath. Do ye think to reap, and never sow? to reap in joy, and never sow in tears? God puts all his children's tears in a bottle; but thou sparest God a labour, because thou never weepest. There are a company that engross all jollity and mirth, as if they had no cause to weep, whose language yet when any man hears, and observes their courses and living in gross sins, he may quickly judge that they of all others have most cause to weep, though there be none more free from mourning, and though they seem to be the only men of the world. But I say to such, go weep, howl, and lament for your sins; for your peace is not yet made with God. Therefore never rest till thou hast got an assurance from heaven that thy sins are forgiven thee. Many people are angry because ministers tell them of this, but surely we must be damned if we do not.

Therefore, as any would hope for comfort, and have God to wipe away their tears from them in another world, let them work upon their hearts here, to shed tears for their own sins first, and then for the sins of the time; for their own first, I say, for a man must first be good in himself before he can be good to others; and then let their grief extend to their brethren even beyond the seas, to the forlorn estate of the church there.

Now the last thing that is noted in Josiah's weeping, is the sincerity of it. 'Thou hast wept *before me*'; that is, sincerely, before God. He sinned before him, and is humbled before him. There is nothing hid from his sight, not only open sins, but he knows the very thoughts of our hearts: therefore let us weep before him without hypocrisy. No matter whether the world see it or no; but let us weep before God, as the prophet saith, 'My soul shall weep in secret for you, and mine eyes shall weep, and drop down tears in the night season' (*Jer.* 13:17). Let us weep in secret before God; for this is without hypocrisy. Now follows the issue of his weeping and humbling of himself.

'I have even heard thee also', saith the Lord.

In which words is set down *God's gracious acceptation of Josiah's humiliation;* which was not without his special observation. 'For I have even heard thee', saith the Lord: so that it seems Josiah did utter some words of grief, because God saith, 'I have *heard it.*' And we may the rather think so, because usually God's children do in their prayers add words unto their tears, as David and good Hezekiah did. Howsoever then his prayer was not a distinct prayer of a composed tenor of speech; yet it was a prayer, because that with these tears he did send up sighs, and groans, and uttered broken words from a broken heart. There was such a language in his heart that

God did understand, for God understands the language of his own Spirit in the hearts of his children. The Spirit knows what we mean, as *Rom.* 8:26–27. God hath an ear to hear our desires, our sighs and groans; for tears have the weight of a voice, they speak for us. Where there is true grief, many times there cannot come a composed tenor of speech; for a broken heart expresseth itself more in sighs, groans, and tears, than in words. Though we do not utter distinct words in a form of prayer, yet he hears our sighs and groans: his ears are open to the cries of his children. So we learn from hence, for our comfort against all Satan's temptations,

*Doct.* 6. *That God takes a particular notice, and understands the prayers we make unto him:* he hears the groans of his children. So David saith, 'My groaning is not hid from thee' (*Psa.* 38:9). So the prophet says, 'He will fulfil the desire of them that fear him; he will also hear their cry, and will save them' (*Psa.* 145:19); yea, he knows our thoughts long before. This must needs be so.

*Reason* 1. First, Because he is gracious and merciful; he is a God hearing prayers.

2. Because of the relations which in his love he hath taken upon himself, to be a Father. So that when a man shall, by the Spirit of adoption, call God Father,

there is such a deal of eloquence and rhetoric in this very word, it works so upon the bowels[6] of God, that he cannot choose but hear. Even as a child, when he speaks to his father, and calls him by this name, this word father doth so work upon him that he cannot but hear. So it is with God; when he hears us call him Father, he cannot but hear us.

3. Because of his nature and love, which is above the love of an earthly father. Though a mother should forget, and not hear her child, yet the Lord will hear us.

And likewise this is his promise: 'Call upon me in the day of trouble, and I will hear thee, and thou shalt glorify me' (*Psa.* 50:15).

4. Again, God cannot basely esteem of our prayers, because they are the motions of his own Spirit. Oh, but they are broken prayers. It is true; but the Spirit understands them and makes intercession for us, with sighs and groans that cannot be expressed; and none can understand them but the Spirit (*Rom.* 8:26–27).

5. Again, God cannot but hear our prayers, because they are offered up in the name of a mediator. They are perfumed with the incense and sacrifice of his Son. Therefore he cannot but hear them.

---

[6] 'Bowels', a term often used in Scripture to refer to the 'seat of the affections'.

6. Again, God must needs hear our prayers, because they are made according to his will. When we pray for ourselves, and for the church of God, it is according to God's will. So then, if we consider these respects, God cannot but hear our prayers.

*Obj.* But some will object, God doth not hear me: I have prayed a long while, and yet he hath not given me an answer.

*Ans.* 1. I answer, God doth always hear, though he seemeth not to hear sometimes, to increase our importunity. Christ heard the woman of Canaan at first; but yet, to increase her importunity, he gave her the repulse and denial, and with the same, inward strength to wrestle with him.

*Ans.* 2. Again, God seems not to hear, because he delights in the music of his children's prayers. Oh how he loves to hear the voice of his children! As a Father to hear the language of his child, though it be none of the best; so it is sweet music in God's ears to hear the prayers of his children. He will have prayers to be cries. Therefore he defers to hear; but in deferring he doth not defer, for he increaseth our strength, as in Jacob's wrestling, that we might cry after him, wrestle with him, and offer violence unto him again.

*Ans.* 3. And sometimes, indeed, he will not hear us, because, it may be, there is some secret Achan in the camp, or some Jonah in the ship; some sin, I mean, in the heart unrepented of; for in this case we may come before God again and again, and he not hear us. This is the reason why God hears not many Christians, because they have not made a thorough inquisition into their own estates, found out their sins and humbled themselves for them. Thus we see for what reasons God defers to hear our prayers.

*Use* 1. If this be so, that God doth hear us, let us make this use to be plentiful in prayers, and lay up a great store of them in the bosom of God, for this is that will do us the most good. He hears everyone in due time. We do never lose a sigh, a tear, or anything that is good, which proceeds from his own Spirit, but he will answer abundantly in his own time. For he that gives a desire, and prepares our heart to pray, and gives us a Mediator by whom to offer them up, will doubtless accept of them in his own Son, and will answer them. The time will come when he will accept of nothing else, and we shall have no other thing to offer up. What a comfort will it then be, that we have in former times, and can now call upon God! The day is coming when goods will do us no good, but prayers will. What a comfort then is it to a Christian, that he hath a God to go to, that hears his prayers! Let all the world join together against a

Christian, take away all things else and cast him into a dungeon, yet they cannot take away his God from him. What a happiness is it to pray! We can never be miserable so long as we have the Spirit of prayer. Though we were in a dungeon with Jeremiah, or in the whale's belly with Jonah, yea, though in hell, yet there we might have cause of comfort.

Let us therefore be ashamed of our barrenness in this duty, and observe whether God hear our prayers, or else how can we be thankful? There be many that pray, because their consciences do force them to some devotion, and therefore they slubber over a few prayers that their consciences may not smite them, but they never observe the issue of their prayers, whether God hears them or not; whereas God is a God hearing prayers, and the child of God doth esteem of nothing but that which he hath from God, as a fruit of prayer, and therefore accordingly he doth return thanks. God will have his children beg all of him. As some fathers will give nothing to their children, but they will have them first ask it of them, so God will give us nothing but what we pray for. And though he doth exceed to give us more than we ask, yet he looks that we should return thanks in some measure proportionable to the benefit received. Therefore let us observe how God hears our prayers, that so we may be suitably thankful. This will strengthen our faith in evil times when we can thus plead with God. Hear, Lord! Heretofore I came before thee, though weakly, yet with a broken heart, and thou didst hear me then. Thou art still a God hearing prayer, therefore, Lord, look upon my estate now and help me. Seeing, then, God hears our prayers, let us think of this glorious privilege, that we have liberty to go to the throne of grace in all our wants. The whole world is not worth this one privilege. We cannot command the prince's ear at all times; but we have a God always to go to, that will hear us. What a wretched folly is it therefore of those that, by their sins, bring themselves into such a condition that they cannot have God to hear them.

*Quest.* But how shall we make such prayers as God will hear?

*Ans.* I answer first of all, Would we be in such an estate that we may enjoy this blessed privilege, to have God's ear ready to hear?

1. First, Then hear him. If we will have God to hear us, then let us hear God, as Josiah did. When he heard the word read, his heart melted. For 'he that turneth away his ears from hearing the law, even his prayers shall be abominable', saith God (*Prov.* 28:9).

And is it not good reason, think we, for God not to hear us, when we will not hear him? 'Because I have called, and you have refused; when you are in misery, and shall out of self-love cry to me to be delivered, then I will refuse to hear you', saith the Lord (*Prov.* 1:24–28). Therefore let all profane persons, that will not hear God, know a time will come, that though they cry and roar, yet he will not hear them.

2. Secondly, If we will have God hear our prayers, they must proceed from a broken heart. Prayers be the sacrifice of a broken spirit. Josiah had a tender and broken heart, and therefore God could not despise his prayers. So David pleads with God: ' The sacrifice of God is a broken and a contrite spirit' (*Psa.* 51:17). So holy Bernard saith, 'I have led a life unbefitting me; but yet my comfort is, that a broken heart and a contrite spirit, Lord, thou wilt not despise.'[7] God will hear the prayers and tears of relenting hearts.

3. Thirdly, To strengthen our prayers we must add to them the wings of love, faith, hope, and earnestness, as Josiah did here. Out of love to his country his prayers were joined with weeping, and he wrestled with tears. Oh! the prayers that have tears with them cannot go without a blessing.

[7] In his Letters very often.

4. Lastly, If we would have God to hear us, let us have such a resolution and purpose of reformation as Josiah had; for his prayers were joined with a purpose of reformation, which he afterwards performed in so strict a manner, that there was never such a reformation among all the kings of Judah as he made. To this purpose David saith, 'If I regard wickedness in my heart, God will not hear my prayer' (*Psa.* 66:18). If we have but a resolution to live in any sinful course, let us make as many prayers as we will, God will not respect them. God regarded good Josiah because he had no purpose to live in any sin against him.

If we come with a traitorous mind unto God, with our sins in our arms, we must look for no acceptation from him. When a man comes to a king to put up a petition unto him, and comes with a dagger in his hand to stab him, will the king accept of this man's petition? So, do we think that God will hear our prayers when we bring a dagger in our hand, to stab him with our sins? If we will not leave swearing, lying, pride, covetousness, and the like, if we have not covenanted with our own hearts, but still go on in sin, we shall never go away with a blessing. Josiah reformed himself; therefore God saith, 'I have also heard thee.' Thus if our prayers issue from a heart rightly affected, as good Josiah's was, then we shall speed as he did; for God did not only hear his prayer, but see how he rewards him with an excellent blessing; to be taken home to heaven from the troubles of this life: which we shall in the next place speak of.

# 4

---

# THE SAINT'S REFRESHING

*Behold, I will gather thee to thy fathers, and thou shalt be gathered to thy grave in peace, neither shall thine eyes see all the evil that I will bring upon this place, and upon the inhabitants of the same. So they brought the king word again.*

2 Chron. 34:28

IT is for the most part the privilege of a Christian, that his last days are his best; and 'though weeping be in the evening, yet joy comes in the morning' (*Psa.* 30:5); though he do begin in darkness, yet he ends in light. Whereas, on the contrary, the wicked begin in jollity and light, but end in darkness; yea, such a darkness as is 'utter darkness' (*Matt.* 8:12)—by Peter called the 'blackness of darkness' (2 *Pet.* 2:17)—the preparations whereunto are, God's outward judgments in this life inflicted upon the impenitent and rebellious, wherein God many times puts a sensible, visible difference betwixt the godly and the wicked; as betwixt Lot and the Sodomites, Noah and the adulterous world, Moses and the Israelites with him, from Korah, Dathan, and his company, the Egyptians and the Israelites at the Red Sea; and in this text, betwixt this good king and his people. He must not see all the evil that God was to bring upon his wicked and rebellious subjects. Oh the happiness of holiness, which is sure to speed well in all storms whatsoever; because on all the glory there is a defence, as Isaiah speaks (*Isa.* 4:5). Light is sown for the righteous (*Psa.* 97:11); and whatsoever his troubles be, yet his last end shall be blessed. 'Let me die', saith Balaam, 'the death of the righteous, and let my last end be like his' (*Num.* 23:10). Such honour have all his saints, such honour had this good king Josiah; being removed from hence that he might not see the evil to come. Though he were taken from earth, yet it was for his good, that he might be gathered into heaven, and make a royal exchange.

The words contain *a promise of a reward, and great favour unto good king Josiah,* that he should die, and be gathered unto his fathers; and that which is more, the manner considered, that he should 'die in peace'; the ground whereof is showed unto him: 'Because thine eyes shall not see all the evil that I will bring upon this place, and upon the inhabitants of the same.' God's promises are of three sorts. First, Such as he made upon condition of legal obedience: 'Do this and thou shalt live.' Secondly, When we are humbled upon sight of our sins, then he propounds another way, and promises that if we believe in Jesus Christ our surety, who hath made satisfaction for us, then we shall live. This is the grand promise of all, the promise of life everlasting, and pardon of sin. Thirdly, There are promises of encouragement unto us, when we are in the state of grace. As a father, who means to make his son an heir, doth give him many promises of encouragement, so God deals with his children, when they are in the covenant of grace.

There are, I say, promises of particular rewards to encourage them, as they are sure of the main and great reward, namely, everlasting life. Therefore, Josiah being an heir of heaven, God did propound a promise of encouragement unto him, by way of favour, to show that his good works were not unregarded. In general here,

*Doct.* 1. First, We may observe *God's gracious dealing with his children,* that he takes notice of every good thing they do, and doth reward them for it, yea, in this life. There is not a sigh but God hears it, not a tear but he hath a bottle for it. Most men spare God a labour in this kind. He promiseth 'to wipe away all tears from our eyes' (*Rev.* 21:4), but they will shed none. Yet the least tear shed, and word spoken in a good cause, goes not without a reward from God; not so much as a cup of cold water, but he rewards. Which must needs be so:

Because God looks upon the good things we do, being his own works in us, as upon lovely objects, with a love unto them; for though Josiah had said nothing, yet his deep humiliation itself, was as it were a prayer, that cried strongly in the ears of God, that he could not but reward it. So that partly because God looks upon us as lovely objects, he loving the work of his own Spirit, and partly because they cry unto God, as it were, and pluck down a blessing from heaven, they cannot go unrewarded.

*Use*. This is matter of comfort, that God will not only reward us with heaven, but will also recompense every good thing we do, even in this world; yea, such is his bounty, he rewards hypocrites. Because he will not be beholding to them for any good thing they do, nor have them die unrewarded, he recompenseth them with some outward favours, which is all they desire. Ahab did but act counterfeit humiliation, and he was rewarded for it (*1 Kings* 21:27-29). So the Scribes and Pharisees did many good things, and had that they looked for. They looked not for heaven, but for the praise of men. This they had, as Christ tells them, 'Verily, I say unto you, you have your reward' (*Matt.* 6:5). God will be beholding to none; but whosoever do anything that is good, they shall have some reward, whether they be good or bad. If the conscience of a man did judge well, he might come to God with boldness, not to brag of good works, but out of an humble heart saying, 'Remember me, O Lord, as I have dealt with thee.' So good Hezekiah did: 'Remember, Lord, how I have walked before thee in truth' (*Isa.* 38:3). When we labour in all our actions to please God, we may with boldness approach to the throne of grace, and say with Peter, Remember, Lord, 'Thou knowest that I love thee' (*John* 21:15). If there were no other reward but this, that we have a privilege to go to God with boldness, our conscience not accusing us, it were enough. What a shame is it, then, that we should be so barren in good works, seeing our labour shall not be unrewarded of the Lord! Oh then let us take counsel of the apostle: 'Finally, my brethren, be ye stedfast and unmoveable, abounding in the work of the Lord, knowing that your labour is not in vain in the Lord' (1 Cor. 15:58). He hath a reward for every cup of cold water, for every tear. Every good deed we do hath the force of a prayer to beg a blessing; yea, our very tears speak loud to God, although we say nothing. But to come to particulars.

'Behold, I will gather thee to thy fathers, *etc.*'

Here we see this word *behold,* a word serving to stir up attention, set before the promise, which was formerly set before a threatening, 'Behold, I will bring evil upon this place, *etc.*' Behold is as necessary before promises as threatenings. For the soul is ready to behold that which is evil, and by nature is prone to dejection, and to cast down itself. Therefore there need be a 'behold' put before the promise, to raise up the dejected soul of Josiah or others, and all little enough. Christians should have two eyes, one to look upon the ill, the other upon the good, and the grace of God that is in them, that so we may be thankful. But they for the most part look only upon the ill that is in them, and so God wants his glory and we our comfort.

'Behold, I will gather thee to thy fathers, and thou shalt be gathered to thy grave in peace.'

*Doct.* 2. Mark here the language of Canaan, *how the Spirit of God in common matters doth raise up the soul to think highly of them.*

Therefore it is that the Holy Ghost sweetens death with a phrase of 'gathering'. Instead of saying, Thou shalt die, he saith, 'Thou shalt be gathered.' How many phrases have we in Scripture that have comfort wrapped in them, as there is in this phrase, 'Thou shalt be gathered to thy grave in peace.' I will not speak how many ways peace is taken in Scripture. 'Thou shalt die in peace'; that is, thou shalt die quietly, honourably, and peaceably. And thou shalt not see the misery that I will bring upon the state and kingdom. Thou shalt be gathered to thy fathers, which is meant to Abraham, Isaac, and Jacob, and to all the faithful patriarchs.

*Doct.* 3. Only observe, it is a very sweet word, and imports unto us, *that death is nothing but a gathering,* and presupposeth that God's children are all scattered in this world amongst wicked men, in a forlorn place, where they are used untowardly, as pilgrims use to be in a strange land. Therefore we had need be gathered, and it is a comfort to be gathered. But from whence shall he be gathered? He shall be gathered from a wicked, confused world; and to whom shall he go?

To his Father.[1] His soul shall go to their souls, his body shall be laid in the grave with theirs. As if he had said, Thou shalt leave some company, but go to better; thou shalt leave a kingly estate, but thou shalt go to a better kingdom.

*Doct.* 4. *The changes of God's children are for the better.* Death to them is but a gathering. This gathering doth show the preciousness of the thing gathered; for God doth not use to gather things of no value. Josiah was a pearl worth the gathering. He was one of high esteem, very precious. So every Christian is dearly bought, with the blood of Christ. Therefore God will not suffer him to perish, but will gather him before the evil days come. As men use to gather jewels before fire comes into their houses; or as husbandmen will be sure to gather their corn, before they will let the beasts come into the field; so saith God to him, I will be sure to gather thee before I bring destruction upon the land. We are all by nature lost in Adam, and scattered from God, therefore we must be gathered again in Christ. For all gathering that is good is in him; for he is the head of all union that is good. And this is to be wrought by the ordinances of God, by the means of the ministry, which is appointed unto that end to gather us, as *Matt.* 23:37, Christ speaks

[1] Or 'fathers'?

to Jerusalem, 'How often would I have gathered you together, as a hen gathereth her chickens under her wings, but you would not.' Christ would have gathered them unto himself, by his word, but they refused.

All the gathering of a Christian in this life is a gathering to Christ by faith, and to the communion of saints by love (*1 Thess.* 4:17); and the more he doth grow in grace, the more near communion he hath with Christ. Then after this gathering by grace, there comes by death a gathering to Christ in glory. For the soul goes for ever and ever to be with the Lord. After this comes a higher degree of gathering at the day of judgment, when there shall be a great meeting of all saints, and the soul and body shall be reunited together, to remain for ever with the Lord. Let us then think of this, that whatsoever befalls us in the world, we shall be sure to be gathered, for death is but a gathering. For from whence goes Josiah? From a sinful world, a sinful estate, a wretched people, unto his fathers, who are all good, nay, to God his Father. We are all here as Daniel in the lion's den, as sheep among wolves; but at death we shall be gathered to our fathers. It is a gathering to a better place, to heaven; and to better persons, to fathers, where we shall be for ever praising the Lord, never offending him, loving and pleasing one another. Here Christians displease one another, and cannot be gathered together in love and affection, but there they shall be gathered in unity of love for ever.

*Use.* This serves, first of all, *to comfort us in departure of friends,* to render their souls up with comfort into the hands of God. We know they are not lost, but sent before us. We shall be gathered to them, they cannot come to us. Therefore why should we grieve? They are gathered in quietness and rest to their fathers. This should also make us render our souls to God, as into the hands of a faithful Creator and Redeemer. From whence go we? From a sinful world and place of tears, to a place of happiness above expression. Why should we be afraid of death? It is but a gathering to our fathers. What a comfort is it to us in this world, that we shall go to a place where all is good, where we shall be perfectly renewed, made in the image of God, and shall have nothing defaced? Let this raise up our dead and drowsy souls. Thus we shall be one day gathered. The wicked shall be gathered together, but a woeful gathering is it. They shall be gathered like a bundle of tares, to be thrown into hell, there for ever to burn. They are dross and chaff, never gathered to Christ by faith, nor to the body of the church by love; and therefore they are as dross and chaff, which the wind scatters here, and shall for ever be scattered hereafter (*Psa.* 1:4). They are, as Cain, vagabonds in regard of the life of grace here; and therefore shall be for ever scattered from the life of glory hereafter. They shall be gathered to those whom they delighted in, and kept company with, whilst they were in this world. They loved to keep company with the wicked here, therefore they shall be gathered to them in hell hereafter. This is sure, thou shalt live in heaven or hell afterwards, with those whom thou livedst with here. Dost thou live only delighted in evil company now? It is pity thou shouldst be severed from them hereafter. If thou be gathered to them in love and affection here, thou shalt be gathered to them in hell and destruction hereafter. It is a comfortable evidence to those that delight in good company, that they shall be with them in heaven for ever. 'Hereby we know that we are translated from death to life, because we love the brethren' (*1 John* 3:14). And on the contrary, those that are brethren in evil here, may read in their own wicked courses and conversation what will become of them hereafter. They are all tares, and shall be gathered together in a bundle, and cast into hell fire for ever.

'And thou shalt be gathered to thy grave in peace.'

Here is a reward, not only to die, but to die in peace. Josiah goes the way of all flesh; he must die though he be a king. This statute binds all. All are liable to death. 'And thou shalt be gathered, or put in thy grave in peace.' This doth declare that he should be buried; the ground whereof is out of *Gen.* 3:19, 'Dust thou art, and to dust thou shalt return.' From earth we came, and to earth we shall return. The earth we carry and the earth we tread on shall both meet together. In that God doth here promise it to Josiah as a blessing, we may hence learn,

*Doct.* 5. *That burial is a comely and honourable thing,* and that we ought to have respect unto it, partly because the body of a dead Christian is a precious thing. They are temples of the Holy Ghost, members of Christ, and therefore ought to have the honour of burial: partly because it shows our love and affection to the party buried, for it is the last kindness we can do unto them. Again, we ought to have respect to burial, to show our hope of the resurrection, that though the body be cast into the earth, yet it shall rise; though it be sown in dishonour, yet it shall rise in honour. So we see that for these reasons burial is honourable. Therefore it is said of the faithful in Scripture, that they were buried, to show how honourable a thing it is; and indeed it is an honour, specially for fathers, to be buried by their friends and children, and carried by them into their graves. For to be buried like a beast is a judgment to wicked men.

*Quest.* But what then shall we say to all those that are not thus buried, whose bodies are given to be torn by wild beasts, or burnt to ashes, or flung into rivers, as antichrist useth to deal with many saints?

*Ans.* I answer that in this case faith must raise itself above difficulty; for though it be a favour and blessing of God, to have Christian burial after we are dead, yet Christians must be content to go without this blessing sometimes when God calls them to the contrary, as when we cannot have it upon good terms, with peace of conscience, or with God's love. In this case a burial in regard of God's favour is not worth the naming. Therefore let all Christians be content to put their bodies, life and all, to hazard; not only to be willing to want burial when we are dead, but to sacrifice our lives and whatsoever else for God, as many saints have been martyred, and their bodies burnt to ashes. Yet God will gather together the ashes of the dead bodies of his children; for 'right precious in the sight of the Lord is the death of his saints' (*Psa.* 116:15). And is it not better to want this with God's favour, than to have the most honourable burial in the world on evil terms? For what saith the Spirit of God? 'Happy and blessed are they which die in the Lord' (*Rev.* 14:13); not happy are they that die in pomp, and are buried in state, but happy are they that die in the Lord. Therefore when we may not have it, although it be a comely thing, yet if we have God and Christ, we have all that is good. Therefore it is no matter what becomes of our bodies after we are dead; for though we be flung into the sea, burnt to ashes, yet both sea and earth must give up all the dead, as it is *Rev.* 20:13. Therefore as for our bodies, let us be willing that God may have them, who gave them; and if he will have us to sacrifice our lives for him, let us do it willingly.

'And thou shalt be gathered to thy grave in peace.'

*Obj.* How is this? for we read, in the succeeding chapter of Josiah, that he died a violent death; he was slain by the hands of his enemies. Is this to die in peace?

*Sol.* I answer, the next words do expound it. He died in peace, 'because his eyes should not see the evil that God would bring upon the land afterwards'; as if he had said, Thou shalt not see the ruin of the church and commonwealth. So, though Josiah were slain by idolaters, by Pharaoh and his chariots, yet he died in peace comparatively with a worse state of life. For though he died a bloody death by the hands of his enemies, yet he died in peace, because he was prevented by death from seeing that which was worse than death. For God may reserve a man in this life to worse miseries than death itself.

From hence we learn this instruction,

*Doct. 6. That death may be less miserable than the ill which a man may live to see in this life; or, that the miseries of this life may be such as that death may be much better than life, and far rather to be chosen.* We may fall into such miseries whilst we do live, that we may desire death, they being greater than it. The reason hereof is, because that a sudden death, in some respects, is better than a lingering one. One death is better than many deaths, for how many deaths did Josiah escape by this one death! It would have been a death to him if he had lived to see the ruin of the commonwealth, the church of God, and his own sons carried into captivity, to have seen them slain, their eyes plucked out, the temple of God plucked down, and idolatry set up.

We ought then to be careful how to avoid a cursed and miserable estate after death. All the care of wicked men is to avoid death. But they may fall into such an estate in this life that they may wish death, as an heathen emperor once did, who complaining said, 'I have none will do me so much favour as to kill me.'[2] All the desire of atheists is, that they may live. Thou base atheist, thou mayest fall into such an estate as is worse than death, and if that be so terrible, what will that[3] estate be after death? An atheist in this life desires life, Oh that I might not die! But in hell thou wilt desire, Oh that I might die! The time will come that thou shalt desire that which thou canst not abide to hear of now. What desperate folly is it therefore to redeem life with base conditions; not to give it for the gospel when we are called to it. In this case, that base life which we so stand upon, will cost us the loss of our soul for ever in hell, when we shall desire to die.

'Behold, I will gather thee to thy fathers, and thou shalt be put in thy grave in peace.' The Lord saith, he 'will gather'. So we see,

*Doct.* 7. *Our times are in God's hand;* as David saith, 'My times are in thy hand' (*Psa.* 31:15). Our times of coming into the world, continuing in it, and

---

[2] Nero?
[3] 'thine'?

going out of it, are in God's hand. Therefore he saith, 'Thou shalt be put in thy grave in peace.' God hath power of death. Our going and coming is from God; he is the Lord of life and death.

*Use. This is a comfort unto us while we live in this world,* that whilst we live we are not in our own hands, we shall not die in our own time; neither is it in our enemies' hands, but in God's hand. He hath appointed a certain time of our being here in this world. This should tie us to obedience, and to die in hope and faith; because when we die we are but gathered to our fathers, to better company and place than we leave behind us.

Again we see here *that men may outlive their own happiness,* that at last life may be a judgment unto them, because they may see that which is worse than death. How many parents live to see the ruin of their own families! the undoing of their children by their own miscarriage! We see God takes away Josiah, because he will not have him live, as it were, beyond his happiness. We see how tenderly affected God is for the good of his children. He pities them when they are in misery, knows what they are able to bear, and will lay no more upon them than he gives them strength to endure. God knew that Josiah was tender-hearted, and melted at the very threatenings, which if he could not endure to hear against his country, could he ever have endured to have seen the miseries upon his people and country? Surely no. Therefore God will rather gather him to his fathers.

Now this is a wonderful comfort, that many times God will not let us see too great matter of grief. Let us then imitate God, and deal so one with another as God deals with us—the husband with the wife, and the wife with the husband, and the like. Let us not acquaint them with such things as may make them more grieve than is fitting, or they are able to bear. God would not have Josiah to see the misery he brought upon his country, because he knew that he was tenderly disposed, that a little grief would soon overcome him. So let us beware of causing any to grieve, or to let them know things which they are not able to bear.

Again, Seeing this is a grief to a kind and loving father, yea, worse than death, to see the ruin of his child, this should teach all those that are young, to take care that they give no occasion of offence to those that are over them, for to grieve; which will be worse than death unto them. It would have been worse than a death unto Josiah to have seen the ruin of his children. So for those children which have been cherished by their parents in their nonage,[4] it will be worse than death to them in their age to see their children lewd and come to ruin, whereby they bring so much sooner the grey head of their father to the grave in sorrow. These offend against the sixth commandment, which saith, 'Thou shalt not kill.' Let us then rather revive and comfort the heart of those that have been good unto us, and not kill them, or do that which is worse than death unto them.

'Neither shall thy eyes see the misery I will bring upon this people.'

*Doct.* 8. Here we learn again *that it is the sight of misery which works the deepest impression*. It is not the hearing of a thing, but the sight of it, which affecteth most deeply; as in the sacrament, the seeing of the bread broken, and the wine poured out, works a deep impression; and because God knew Josiah's heart would break at the sight of the misery, therefore he tells him, 'Thine eyes shall not see the evil that I will bring upon this place.' The sight is a most working sense, to make the deepest impression upon the soul. What shall be our great joy and happiness in heaven, but that we shall see God for evermore? Sight is a blessing upon earth, both the eyes of the

---

[4] That is, legal infancy, minority: time of immaturity.

body wherewith we see, and the eyes of the soul—that is, faith—which makes us see afar off, till in heaven we shall see him face to face. So that sight makes us both happy and miserable.

*Use* 1. *How wretched, then, is the estate of them that shall see themselves,* with their own wicked eyes, *sent to hell, with the creature they delighted in.* That which the eyes see, the heart feels. There are many atheists, whose whole care is to preserve life. They would live, although they live the life of a dog. But the time will come, that thou wilt more earnestly desire death than life. Thy eyes shall see, and thy body feel, and thy conscience too, that which is worse than a thousand deaths. Thou shalt then die a living death. The worm of thy conscience shall gnaw thee for ever, and shalt see and feel the tormenting fire which shall never be quenched. That which the wicked nourish now to follow their humour, never caring to please God, the day will be when they shall desire to avoid it; and that which they labour to avoid most now, the time will come when they shall most desire it. Death is the king of fears. It is terrible. But then look beyond death: what is behind that? Thou shalt see at the heels of it hell and eternal damnation.

*Use* 2. This should teach us also *how to understand the promise of long life.* It is a promise and a favour of God to be desired. It is a prayer with condition, if God see it good; else God may give us long life, to see and feel a world of misery. Therefore such promises are to be desired conditionally: if God see it good for us.

*Doct.* 9. Again, The Holy Ghost saith here, 'Thy eyes shall not see the evil I will bring upon this place.' Hence we learn, *that those which be dead in the Lord, are freed from seeing of any evil of misery.* The godly shall see no misery after death. If this be so, then they do not go into purgatory after death, as the papists hold. The Holy Ghost saith, Josiah is taken away from seeing any evil to come. Then sure they do not fall into such misery after death, which is worse than death. True, say the papists, such excellent men as Josiah do go to heaven immediately. Ay, but the Holy Ghost saith by Isaiah (57:1), that 'the righteous are taken away from the evil to come.' It is spoken of the whole generation of righteous men. Therefore it is a sottish[5] thing for them to hold that any of them shall see purgatory, when God saith the righteous are taken away from seeing any evil to come.

*Doct.* 10. And as it is against them in this, so *here is another conclusion against popery, that takes away their invocation of saints:* for the righteous go heaven,

---

[5] That is, foolish, stupid.

and cannot see or know our wants and miseries; yeu, they are taken away, because they should not see the miserable estate that befalls their posterity. Then if they do not know our wants, how can they hear and help us when we pray, seeing it is a part of their happiness not to understand our miseries? For if Josiah, from heaven, could have seen the desolation and misery that befell his country afterwards, it would have wrought upon him. But Josiah was taken away, that he should not see it. Therefore, why should men spend that blessed incense and sacrifice of prayer, unto those that cannot hear? But put case, they could hear some; yet can they hear all that pray unto them? A finite creature hath but a finite act and limited power. How can one saint give a distinct answer and help to perhaps a thousand prayers, as the virgin Mary hath many thousand prayers offered her? How can she distinctly know and give a distinct answer to every prayer?

'Thou shalt be put in thy grave in peace, neither shall thy eyes see all the evil that I will bring upon this place.' *Let us learn here a mystery of divine providence in his death;* for there is a mystery of providence, not only in great matters, as election and predestination, but in ordering of the common things of the world. How many excellent mysteries are here wrapt together in this death of Josiah! As, first, it is said that he died in peace, whereas he died a violent death, and was slain by the hands of his enemies. His death was both a mercy and a correction: a correction for his error in being so hasty in going to war with Pharaoh, king of Egypt; and yet it was a mercy, because it prevented him from seeing the evil to come, and so likewise brought him sooner to heaven. It is a strange thing to see how the wisdom of heaven can mingle crosses and favours, corrections and mercies together; that the same thing should be both a mercy to Josiah to be taken away, and yet a correction also for his error, in going to fight against Necho, king of Egypt, as we see 2 *Chron.* 35:21–22. We may have mercies and afflictions upon us at the same time, as God, by the same death, corrected Josiah's folly, and rewarded his humility.

Mark here again another mystery, *in the carriage of divine providence:* how he brings his promises to pass strangely above the reach of man; as here, he having promised Josiah that he should die in peace, one would have thought that Josiah should have died in pomp and state. No. Thou shalt die in peace, although thou be slain by the hand of thy enemies; thou shalt come to heaven, although it be by a strange way. Thus God brings his children to heaven by strange ways, yea, by contrary ways, [by] afflictions and persecutions. Paul knew he should come to Rome, although it were by a strange way; though he suffered shipwreck, and was in great danger, as we may see *Acts* 27. God hath strange ways to bring his counsels to pass, which he doth so strangely, as we may see his own hand in it.

Again, Here we may see another mystery in divine providence, concerning the death of Josiah, *in that he was taken away being a young man,* but thirty-nine years old, who was the flower of his kingdom, and one upon whom the flourishing estate of such a kingdom did depend. Now, for such a gracious prince to be taken away in such a time, and at such an age, when he might have done much good, a man would hardly believe this mystery in divine providence. But 'our times are in God's hand' (*Psa.* 31:15). His time is better than ours. And therefore he, seeing the sins of the people to be so great, that he could not bear with them longer,—for it was the sins of the people that deprived them of Josiah. It was not the king of Egypt who was the cause of his death, but the sins of the land—those caused God to make this way, to take away their gracious king.

*Use.* Here we may admire the wisdom of God,

who doth not give an account unto us of his doings, why he suffers some to live, and takes away others; why he suffers the wicked to live, and takes away his own. We can give little reason for it, because it is a mystery; but God best knoweth the time when to reap his own corn.

'Neither shall thy eyes see all the evil I will bring upon this place, and upon the inhabitants of the land.'

*Doct.* 11. Here the Holy Ghost doth insinuate unto us that whilst Josiah was alive, God would not bring this judgment upon the land, but after his death, then it should come upon them. So here we learn this comfortable point of instruction, *that the lives of God's children do keep back judgment and evil from the place where they live, and their death is a forerunner of judgment.* Their life keeps back ill, and their death plucks down ill. While thou art alive, I will bring no evil upon this place, but when thou art gone, then I will bring it down, saith God. The reasons of this are,

*Reason* 1. *Because gracious men do make the times and the places good where they live.* It is a world of good that is done by their example and help. While they live the times are the better for them.

*Reason 2.* And again, *they keep back ill, because gracious men do bind God by their prayers.* They force, as it were, a necessity upon God, that he must let the world alone. They bind his hands, that he will do nothing while they are in it; as to Lot in Sodom, 'I can do nothing while[6] thou art gone', saith the angel (*Gen.* 19:22). They stand in the gap, and keep God from pouring down the vials of his wrath. But when they are gone, there is nothing to hinder or stop the current of divine justice, but that it must needs have his course. As when men have gathered their corn into their barns, then let their beasts, or whatsoever else go into the field, they care not; and as when the jewels are taken out of a rotten house, though the fire then seize upon it, men regard not. So when God's jewels are gathered to himself, then woe to the wicked world, for then God will break forth in wrath upon them. Woe to the old world when Noah goes into the ark, for then follows the flood. Woe to Sodom when Lot goes out of it, for then it is sure to be burned. Luther prayed that God would not bring war upon the people in Germany all his time, but when he died, the whole land was overspread with war. So, before the destruction of Jerusalem, God did gather the Christians to a little city called Pella,

[6] That is, 'until'.

near Jerusalem, then came Titus and Vespasian and ruinated the city of Jerusalem. So there are many gracious parents that die, after whose death comes some miserable end to their wicked children, but not before. God takes away the parents out of the world, that they might not see the ruin of their children. So then we see that it is clear, that good men keep back judgment from the places where they live.

What should we learn from hence?

*Use* 1. This should teach us *to make much of such men as truly fear God,* seeing it is for their sakes that God doth spare us. They carry the blessing of God with them wheresoever they go. As Laban's house was blessed for Jacob's sake (*Gen.* 30:27), and Potiphar's for Joseph's sake (*Gen.* 39:5), so the wicked are spared and fare the better for the saints who live among them. But what is the common course of wicked men? To hate such with a deadly hatred above all others, because their lives and speeches do discover the wickedness of theirs, and because they tell them the truth, and reprove them.

Therefore it was that Ahab could not endure the sight of Micaiah, that holy prophet, who without flattery spake downright truth (*1 Kings* 22:8ff.). So it is now beyond seas and elsewhere. They labour to root out all the good men. But what will they get by it? Surely it will be a thousand times worse with them than it is, for if they were out, then woe to the land presently.

*Use* 2. This should also teach us *to pray to God to bless those that are good.* Is it not good for us to uphold those pillars whereby we stand? What madness is it for a man to labour to pull down the pillar whereby he is holden alive? As Samson, pulling down the pillars of the house, brought death upon himself, so godly men, the pillars of this tottering world, which uphold the places where they live, being once shaken, all the whole state falls. Therefore let us not be enemies to our own good, to hate the godly; for it is for their sakes the Lord shows mercy to us, and refrains to pour out his judgment upon the wicked world. And when the best gathering of all gatherings shall come, that the elect of God shall be gathered together, then comes the misery of all miseries to the wicked. So we see this point is clear, that the godly, while they are alive, keep back ill and bring much good. For doth God continue the world for wicked men? Surely no. For what glory and honour hath God from such wicked wretches? Do they not swear, lie, live filthily, and abuse his members? Is it for these that God doth continue the world? Surely no; but for the godly's sake are judgments deferred, and the world is continued.

*Use* 3. If this be thus, *well may we lament the death of those that are good*. For when they are gone, our safety is gone. 'They are the chariots and horsemen of Israel' (2 *Kings* 2:12). Therefore well may we bewail their loss. Well might Jeremiah lament for the death of Josiah, for together with the breath of Josiah the life of that state breathed out; together with him, the flourishing condition of Jerusalem died, and lay buried with him as it were in the same grave.

See here again how God correcteth too much resting on the arm of flesh. They blessed themselves under Josiah, as if no evil should come near them; as appears, *Lam.* 4:20, 'The breath of our nostrils, the anointed of the Lord, was taken in their pits, of whom we said, Under his shadow we shall live.' There is no greater wrong to ourselves, and to others on whom we rest so much, than to secure ourselves so much on them as to neglect serious turning to God.

'Neither shall thy eyes see all the evil I will bring upon this place.'

This is the ground why he should die in peace, 'Because he shall not see all the evil I will bring upon this place.' Here we see that the judgment which God threatened to bring upon the church and common-wealth is set down by this word 'evil'. 'Thine eyes shall not see all the evil I will bring upon this place.' But who sends this evil? It is an evil brought by God. Thou shalt not see the evil 'I will bring, *etc.*' It was not God that brought it properly, but Nebuchadnezzar, who carried his sons into captivity. Howsoever, God had a hand in it. 'For is there any evil in the city and God hath not done it?' saith the prophet (*Amos* 3:6). But we must distinguish between evil. There is,

1. The evil of sin; and 2. The evil of punishment.

First, The evil of sin; and this God doth not bring, for it is hateful unto him. Then the evil of punishment, which is twofold:

(1.) Either that which comes immediately from God, as famine, pestilence, or the like; in which punishments we are to deal with God alone.

(2.) Or else, the evil that comes from God, but by men, which he useth as instruments to punish us, and this is by war and cruel usage.

Now thus Josiah is taken away from this greatest evil we can suffer in this life; to have God correct us by the hands of men. For when we have to deal with God, the labour is easier to prevail with him, as David did (2 *Sam.* 24:14). But when we have to deal with merciless men, then we have to deal with the poisoned malice of men, besides God's anger. Now the evil that comes from God is chiefly,

The ill which seizeth upon the soul after death; or else, the evil which seizeth upon the whole man, both soul and body, both in this and after this life.

Thus God is said to bring evil, not the evil of sin, but the evil of punishment.

*Doct.* 12. Hence we learn, that *the evils which we suffer, they are from the evil of sin.* It is sin that makes God to bring evil upon the creature. If we look upward to God, there is no evil in the world, for in that consideration all things are good so far as he hath a hand in them. Therefore, whatsoever the creature suffers, it comes from the meritorious evil, the evil of sin. It comes from God, but through the evil of sin provoking him.

*Quest.* If any man ask, How can God, which is good, bring that which is evil?

*Sol.* I answer, We must know that the evil of punishment is the good of justice. All the evil that he doth is good, as it comes from him in his justice punishing, because it doth good to them that are punished, either to cause them to return, or if they will not, to show the glory of his justice in condemning them. It is the good of justice, and it is not always in God only permitting or suffering such a thing for to be done; but it is in him as an act, having a hand in it.

Therefore God saith, 'Ashur is the rod of my wrath';[7] so that in all punishments God hath a hand, whether it be upon the body or soul.

*Use.* This serves for direction unto us, *To begin where we should begin;* in all our afflictions to go to heaven and make our peace with God, and not go to secondary causes. For all evil of punishment comes from him. Let us, if we fear evil, make our peace with God by repentance and new obedience; and then he will overrule all secondary causes so as to help us. Go not in this case to the jailor, or to the executioner, but go to the judge. Let us make our peace in heaven first, and then there will be soon a command for our ease. Yea, Christ can command the wind and sea to be still, the devil himself to be quiet, if our peace be made with him.

Therefore let us learn this lesson, and not fret against the instrument whereby God useth to correct us. David had learned thus much when Shimei railed upon him: 'It is God that hath bid him, therefore let him alone' (2 *Sam.* 16:11). So holy Job saith, 'It is God that gives, and God that takes away' (*Job* 1:21). He doth not only say, God gives, but God takes away. Oh but it was the Chaldeans that took it away. Ay, but it is no matter for that, God gave

---

[7] That is, 'Assyria'. Cf. *Isa.* 10:5.

them leave. Therefore let us carry ourselves patiently, in all troubles, submitting ourselves under the mighty hand of God, from whom we have all evil of punishment.

*Obj.* Again, Here we have another mystery of divine providence. For it may be objected. What! will God bring evil upon his own church and people? upon the temple and place where his name is called upon, and that by idolaters? Where is divine justice now?

*Sol.* I answer. Hold thy peace, take not the balance out of God's hand. He knows what is better for us than we ourselves. We must not call God to our bar, for we shall all appear before his. God useth servants and slaves to correct his sons; worse men than his people to correct his people. It is his course so to do, when they of his own sin against him. For evil men many times make evil men good, when they are used as instruments to correct them; as here God useth wicked men to make his children good. So God makes a rod of Ashur, to make his evil children better. He useth slaves to correct his sons, because it is too base a service for the angels or good men to do. Therefore he useth the devil and his instruments to do it. Wherefore let us not call into question God's providence; for when he will punish his people, he can hiss for a worse people; for Egypt, or Ashur, or the like. So if he will punish England, he can hiss again for the Danes, or Normans, to punish his own people. Let us not boast we are God's people and they idolaters. No; God can hiss for a baser people to punish his own saints. It is the will of God so to dispose, and the will of God is *summa justitia,* the height of justice. God will have it so. Let us make our peace with him, and not demand why he doth thus and thus.

'And so they brought the king word again.'

I will but touch this in a word, and so make an end.

Here we see that the messengers deal faithfully with Josiah. They brought the direct message which the prophetess did bid them, which was good for himself, but doleful for his estate. He was a gracious man, and God gave him gracious servants.

*Doct.* 13. *For God will give good men faithful servants,* that shall deal faithfully with them. As for the wicked, God will give them such servants that shall humour them to their own ruin. If they have a heart not desirous to hear the truth, if they be Ahabs, they shall have four hundred false prophets to lead them in a course to their own ruin. But

Josiah had an upright heart, desiring to know the truth. Therefore God gave him a faithful prophetess to deal truly with him, and faithful messengers to bring the true answer.

'Then the king sent and gathered together all the elders of Judah and Jerusalem. And the king went up into the house of the Lord, and all the men of Judah, and the inhabitants of Jerusalem, and the priests, and the Levites, and all the people great and small,' *etc.*

Which words show what good king Josiah did upon the receipt of this message. As soon as ever he heard it, he did not suffer it to cool upon him. But when his spirit was stirred up, he did as a gracious king should do, he sent and gathered all the elders of Judah, and the inhabitants of Jerusalem, both great and small, and they went up to the house of the Lord, and there read in their ears all the words of the book of the covenant which was found in the house of the Lord.

Here, first, we see that Josiah gathered, as it were, a parliament and a council; as also, in both Josiah and the people, we may behold an excellent and sweet harmony of state, when all, both king and priests, Levites and people, did meet amiably together.

This was an excellent time, when there was such an harmony between king and people, that he no sooner commands but they obeyed him.

But more particularly we learn,

*Doct.* 14. *That the care of the commonwealth and of the church is a duty belonging to the king,* that the reformation both of church and commonwealth belongs unto the prince. There is a generation which think that the king must only take care for the commonwealth. But they have also power to look to religion. We see Josiah doth it, he is the keeper of both. Josiah hath a care of religion, and it doth become his place. He is a head, and it is befitting his relation. He is a father, not only to look to the temporal state, but to the church.

The Donatists in Augustine's time did ask, What had the emperor to do with the church? But it was answered that the emperor could not rule the commonwealth except he govern the church, for the church is a commonwealth. So that we see, as a chief right, the ordering of the matters of religion belongs to the care of the prince. But there are two things in religion: first, intrinsical, within the church, as to preach, administer the sacraments, and ordain ministers. These he ought not to do. But for those things that are without it, these belong unto him. If any of those that are placed in church or commonwealth, do not their duty, it is fitting for him to correct. He ought to set all a-going without, and to remove abuses, but not to meddle with the things within the church aforesaid, as to execute the same, but to oversee and govern their execution, and those persons whose proper office it is to execute them.

This observe against the usurpation of the pope, and see the supremacy of king Josiah, that he is supreme over all; not only over temporal persons, but over evangelical persons. For there was an high priest at that time and the Levites, but none were above king Josiah.

*Quest.* Ay, but this was under the law, say the papists.

*Sol.* 1. I answer, that this is a rule in divinity, that the gospel doth not take away or dissolve the laws of nature and reason. Therefore if the supremacy belonged to the prince then, surely now much more. Therefore saith one, We give respect to the emperor as next to God; to God in the first place, and then to the emperor.[8] The ministers have power over the prince for to direct him and give him counsel, but yet they are not above him. A physician doth give directions for his patient. Is he therefore above him?

[8] Tertullian. Cf. *Apology*, c. xxxiii to xxxvi.

So a builder giveth direction for the building of the king's house. Is this any supremacy? So the minister may give direction and counsel to the prince; but hath he therefore any superiority above the prince? Surely no.

*Sol.* 2. In the second place, here we see who it is that called this parliament. It was king Josiah. He was the first mover in calling of this council, for he was the head; and had it not been a strange thing to have seen the foot move before the head? The head must first give direction before any of the members can move. Therefore it is only in the authority of the king to gather a council, and none must gather a public assembly without authority from the king.

The calling of assemblies belongs to the prince. If it be a general council, then it must be by the emperor; if it be a national council, then by the king or prince of that nation; if provincial, then first from the king or princes, as first movers of it, and so to others. As the heavens, and these celestial bodies over the earth, first move, and then all other afterward, so kings ought first to move, and then all to follow.

*Use* 1. If this be so, we see how the pope wrongfully takes this right of calling councils to himself, which properly belongs to the emperor; for we know that for a thousand years after Christ the emperor called councils, if any were. But of late years the pope, encroaching upon the emperor, hath usurped this right of calling them, when as you see no assemblies ought to gathered without the authority of the prince.

Though fasting be an excellent thing, yet public fasting must not be without the consent of the king. Let Christians have as much private fasting as they will, thereby to humble themselves, but public fasts must not be without the consent of the king; for great matters are to be done by great motions. Here is a great matter of gathering a council. Therefore the head and body and all join together. As it is when the body is to do some great thing, all the members of the body stir together to do it, so it is with the commonwealth. When great matters are in hand, all must be joined together, as here king, priests, Levites, and all the people, both great and small, joined together for to prevent the judgment threatened.

But what must we do if things be amiss? I answer, Take the right course; go to God by prayer, and entreat him who hath the hearts of kings in his hands, to incline and stir up the hearts of princes for to reform abuses. Well, but what did the king do when he had gathered all the elders and inhabitants of Judah and Jerusalem into the house of the Lord?

They went up thither to fast, and pray, and read the book of the law.

Reformation makes all outward things fall into a good rule, but they are to be called only by the authority of the prince, and when a fit time and occasion requires.

The papists brag much of the Council of Trent; but if ever there was a conspiracy against Christ, it was in that council; for the parties that had most offended, and were most accused, and should have been judged, were the judges; and the Holy Ghost, which should have been in the council, and should have been their judge, him they excluded, and received a foul spirit of antichrist sent unto them, in a cap-case[9] from Rome, whence they had all their counsel. Was not this a goodly council?

Again, In that Josiah gathered a council in time of public disorder and public danger, here we learn that it is not only lawful, but many times necessary, to gather assemblies and councils for reformation of abuses, both in church and commonwealth, which otherwise cannot be abolished. So councils are good to make canons, rules, and to prevent heresy; yea, much good may be done by gathering of them, if they meet to a good end, for the good of the church,

[9] That is, a small case or travelling-box.

and the glory of God; for God who is willing and able to perform the good will be strongly amongst them. For if Christ by his Spirit hath promised to be in that assembly, 'where two or three are gathered together' upon good grounds, and to good ends, how much more will he be, when two or three hundreds are so gathered together? But this must be done by the consent of authority, otherwise it would be an impeachment to government. So much briefly for this text, and for this time.[10]

[10] The frequent allusions in the preceding sermons, and throughout, to wars and accompanying evils abroad, receive interpretation from 'The Thirty Years' War', which, beginning in 1618 and ending in 1648, was thus contemporary with the whole of Sibbes's public life.

ALSO BY RICHARD SIBBES
AVAILABLE FROM
THE BANNER OF TRUTH

## Two Titles in the Puritan Paperbacks Series

### *The Bruised Reed*

In this short exposition of Isaiah 42:1–3 Sibbes unfolds the tender ministry of Jesus Christ, who is a 'physician good at all diseases, especially at the binding up of the broken heart' (p.8). There is comfort here for the weak and hurting Christian, help for the Christian struggling with assurance, and caution to ministers not to seek to be more pure than Christ.

What insight into the tactics of the devil! What a wise balance between comfort at the mercy of Christ and not abusing that mercy! What insight into the unexpected ways in which a Christian triumphs! Perhaps most surprising of all—the aptness of his observations concerning the state of the church, as if this book were written yesterday!

Conrad Pomeroy in *Evangelical Times*

**144pp. Paperback** ISBN 978 0 85151 740 7

### *Glorious Freedom*

Sibbes examines the fuller self-revelation of God in the coming of Christ and its greater effect in those who behold that glory by the Spirit. The vitality of the new covenant brings about spiritual liberty and likeness to Christ.

**208pp. Paperback**
ISBN 978 0 85151 791 9

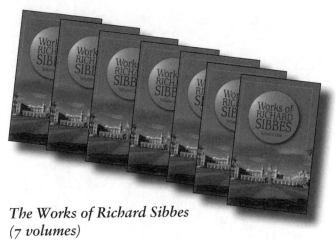

## The Works of Richard Sibbes
### (7 volumes)

Strong thoughts, simple sentences, deep knowledge of the Bible and the human heart, and a sure pastoral touch are here revealed in Sibbes' sustained concentration on the glory and grace of God in Christ.

More than anything else, Sibbes was a great preacher. He never lost sight of the fact that the best Christian counselling is done through the patient and lively exposition of the Word of God. Sibbes excelled as a comforter of the troubled and doubting, but he also possessed the rare gift of illuminating every passage of Scripture he handled by drawing out its significance for his hearers and readers.

The republication of the Nichol edition of his complete works is a notable event for all who have an appetite for helpful and faithful biblical preaching. Volume 1 contains a memoir of Sibbes by A. B. Grosart.

Approx 550pp. per volume   Clothbound
Set ISBN 978 0 85151 398 0